For Bob, with *** *** *** wish
and congratulations on your
new novel.

Warmest regards,
Marion Simon

THE SHOW MUST GO ON

THE SHOW MUST GO ON

My Dance with Chicago

MARION ELISBERG SIMON

HARLED, LLC
Chicago, IL

Published by
HARLED, LLC
Chicago, IL

Publisher's Cataloging-in-Publication Data
Simon, Marion Elisberg.

    The show must go on : my dance with Chicago / by Marion Elisberg Simon. – Chicago, IL : Harled, LLC, 2012.

    p. ; cm.

    ISBN13: 978-0-9860242-0-7

    1. Simon, Marion Elisberg. 2. Fund-raisers (Persons)— United States—Biography. 3. Women—Illinois—Chicago— Biography. I. Title.

    HV41.9.U5 S56 2012
    658.15224—dc23   2012948948

Project coordination by Jenkins Group, Inc.
www.BookPublishing.com

Interior design by Brooke Camfield

Printed in the United States of America
16   15   14   13   12 • 5   4   3   2   1

Dedication

Dedicated to my mother, Lillian,
and my daughters, Kathleen Marion and Toni Celeste

CONTENTS

Foreword

Marion Elisberg Simon was born into the rarefied realms where society and social work alchemize into the kind of fund-raising that could be experienced as *partyosis extrordinarosis*. A successful philanthropist rainmaker with more than ninety years of unique experiences, Marion has spent most of the twentieth century and a good part of the twenty-first turning problems into solutions and social needs into a ball—literally.

Marion is so ingrained in the fabric of Chicago that one would be hard-pressed to find an area of concern in which this petite nonagenarian dynamo hasn't somehow been involved in its improvement. From health care, child care, education, and the arts to architectural preservation and public housing, Marion's commitment, energy, tenacity, and spirit bear a silent but accomplished witness throughout our great city. Chicago anchors such as the University of Chicago, the Chicago Youth Centers, the Medical Research Institute Council (MRIC) at Michael Reese Hospital, the Lincoln Park Zoo, and Roosevelt University have benefited from her gracious talent for tapping into very deep pockets.

Like nearly all "A-list" fund-raisers, Marion belongs to a special breed of American women. She was given, as were others like her, lessons in elegance as well as a college education—at the University of Chicago, no less—when, at the time, high school was considered higher education for women.

In addition to fulfilling her role as a wife, mother, and daughter, Marion worked hard for a variety of charitable causes, usually through the creation of an "event" and without the expectation of being paid for her efforts. She employed all of her connections, manners, education, and energy to create many memorable soirees and succeeded at her job of raising money for numerous charities.

Marion is unique in many ways. Although she would not describe herself as a feminist, she has witnessed enormous change in the roles of women, been at the front of various trends, and supported and mentored other women along the way. However, her life has often been plagued by challenges that could have broken a lesser woman. But no matter how difficult things got, Marion managed to straighten her back, raise her head, and find a reason to face the day with a smile.

The first time I met Marion was at the Coq d'Or restaurant in the Drake Hotel. She was wearing a beautiful knit suit, pearls, understated heels, and a broad smile. Nearly seventy at the time, she could have passed for fifty. Beautiful, elegant, and unbelievably tiny, Marion displayed what I now know to be her characteristic warmth and genuine interest in others, a combination of qualities that makes those in her presence relaxed enough to engage with her and reveal themselves.

I was so relaxed that I nearly forgot the purpose of our meeting: an evaluation of me. At the time, Marion was on the board of Michael Reese Hospital and had raised $75,000 to produce a one-hour program teaching inner-city children how to avoid contracting the AIDS virus.

Marion didn't flinch at the stark realities of the tough situation or shrink from the challenge to educate the public—and the children—on what needed to be done. She also didn't hesitate to say no to ideas she didn't like, yet she listened carefully to my thoughts while quietly evaluating me, never losing her polite smile in the process.

I got the job. With a cast of talented young actors, an amazing on-camera educator, and a finale in which we changed the old Staple Singers song "Respect Yourself" into lyrics celebrating the empowering notion "Protect Yourself," we created an important program that I am extremely proud of two decades later.

Somehow Keith Pochter, who was on the MRIC board with Marion and was brought into the mix, got Audrey Hepburn to agree to be the on-camera host. The show became my first national program and went on to win a Corporation for Public Broadcasting Gold Award for excellence in the informational category.

In addition to working with her on this important project, from my friend Marion I have learned that successful fund-raising requires a dance both intricate and intimate. There is a delicate rhythm to knowing what to ask, how to ask, and what to ask for—and Marion seems to have mastered it all (maybe due to her experience at a young age performing on stage throughout the city).

While Marion describes fund-raising mostly as a game of matching people with their passions, the choreography is far more complicated. It is, in fact, a ballet of imagination, grace, dignity, contacts, listening skills, leadership, and chutzpah. This is the story of a woman with all those qualities as well as enthusiasm and energy to spare.

Marion's life is a lesson in perseverance and determination. Gifted with beauty, brains, ambition, a sense of humor, and an appreciation for all that life has to offer, she used each one of those gifts to survive the slings and arrows of her sometimes tremendously heartbreaking misfortune. She is one of Chicago's grandest dames—an inspiration to us all—and our city wouldn't be the same without her.

—Terry Spencer Hesser

ACKNOWLEDGMENTS

My thanks to my special friend, Josephine Strauss, who is ultimately the one responsible for my writing this book. She and I would discuss some of my life experiences, and she would say, "You really have to write a book!" This was followed by discussions with my talented friend Terry Spencer Hesser, who had already written a few books, and she began to write down my history as I dictated it. My brilliant friend Kristi Peterson was so interested in the book she pushed me to keep doing it and then surprised me by finding Jerrold Jenkins's publishing company, the Jenkins Group, in Traverse City, Michigan. What a pleasant discovery!

I told only a few close friends about the book, and they were very excited and immediately supportive: Mary O'Leary, one of my very best friends, from my days at Michael Reese Hospital; Margo Morris, a close friend from the Lincoln Park Zoo; and Pam Sheffield, whom I had worked with on many committees and one of the loveliest women I know in Chicago. My friends Don Raney and Jaymes Richardson—both very creative—helped me with my ninetieth birthday celebration and were the ones who gathered the photos that we used throughout the book. Stan Lewin, my very dear friend, helped with his wonderful critique of the book.

When I reached the last stages of publishing my memoir, I was ready to tell more of my friends and family about my plans to write a book about me and Chicago. My long-standing Lincoln Park Zoo friend Ron Culp bolstered me from the beginning and has arranged for me to have Sylvie Sadarnac, a talented PR professional, do all the publicity and introductory arrangements for the book. They are both extremely bright.

I thank Christine Mallul for helping to facilitate the donation of proceeds from the sale of this book to the Lincoln Park Zoo. I am excited to be able to give back to the zoo in this new way.

My thanks to Jerrold Jenkins for his faith in me—I am most appreciative. Thank you to Devon Ritter, my editor (University of Chicago Press), for her excellent guidance and enthusiastic support at all times. My special thanks to my dear friends Ramsey Lewis, Bill Zwecker, Bill Kurtis, and President Charles Middleton of Roosevelt University for their helpful comments.

All of my friends and acquaintances, as they gradually began to learn about the book, have been excited and encouraging and thoroughly kind. I thank everyone!

INTRODUCTION

Chicago is my city! I was born here in 1918 and still live in the magnificent metropolis nearly a century later. My involvement in the "Windy City" has spanned a large part of the twentieth century, and even some of the twenty-first, and includes many thrills and successes as well as challenges and disappointments. From the University of Chicago, Cabrini-Green, and Michael Reese Hospital in the south part of the city to the Red Cross, Lincoln Park Zoo, and Roosevelt University downtown, I've worked to improve many important aspects all throughout my beloved city.

I've traveled the world both personally and professionally, but Chicago will always be my home, and I do love it here. Its unique appeal makes it at once quiet but exciting, large but close-knit, clean but gritty. A treasured jewel on the lake, its downtown boasts some of the world's best cultural institutions, and the city has become only more beautiful over the years, with its lush gardens and bountiful and colorful flowers. I've seen my share of the city's changes and growth, paralleling many of my own life's experiences. Chicago and I have grown up together.

All of my accomplishments and achievements in my life and for my city benefited from the lessons I learned during my stage experience as a young girl and into my teen years: the show must go on! No matter what life throws at you, you lift your head up, take a deep breath, and keep going. I've had my share of trials and tribulations, but I've always done what I do best: persevere.

PART I

MY CHILDHOOD CHRONICLE

Ancestral Births and Beginnings

I was born on August 19, 1918, at Jackson Park Hospital on Chicago's South Side. The first five years of my life, I lived near Washington Park, and then my family moved near Jackson Park when we resided in Hyde Park. I would remain a resident of the South Side for nearly a quarter of a century. Most of my world growing up was within Hyde Park's boundaries, including the south end of Lake Michigan and its beaches, as well as Promontory Point.

When I was born on August 19, 1918, everyone was taken with my big eyes. My father said, "You should see her! She's so smart!"

1

During that time, children freely visited their neighbors and went in and out of every building on their block to explore the day's happenings. I was no exception. An only child, I also thrived on my imagination. My collection of dolls, including a life-size walking doll named Dorothy, a mechanical baby doll that crawled, and imported French and Italian dolls, was my source of entertainment as well as companionship. I had a make-believe friend named Jersey, and my one good friend in the neighborhood, Marjorie Sachs, lived across the court from my family's apartment. When we couldn't go outside to play, we waved to each other from our bedroom windows.

I was an only child but often played with my cousins. Here I'm shown with Edgar (right) and Arnold (left) Drucker.

My parents gave me the attention I needed—but I wasn't spoiled in any sense of the word. However, I did know my prominent place in the family. At two years old, when introduced to our Czechoslovakian housekeeper, Anna, I remember telling her, "You know, I'm the most important person here!" Anna and I would play in Jackson Park and visit the Golden Lady statue, a replica from the World's Columbian Exposition. Betty von Chia, our family's Chow dog, went everywhere with us. It was a fun, safe time, and I remember my childhood, and my parents, fondly.

My parents, both of whom were born in Chicago, were first-generation Americans and embodied the hard work, courage, determination, and self-reliance (and reliance on each other) that typified the American dream. My mother, Lillian, was an intellectually gifted and attractive woman who would live to be 106 years old. Unfortunately, she spent many of those years lying in dark rooms while fighting the crippling pain of migraine headaches or surrendering to an even more debilitating depression that doctors later determined may have been triggered by a series of allergies.

Keenly competent and bright but deprived of the education offered to male children, she enrolled in secretarial school and later secured a job as an administrative assistant to the head of Bethlehem Steel during World War I. During this time she met my father, Harry, a gentle man in every way. Kind, well liked, and nothing but perfectly pleasant, he would use his delightful demeanor to win my mother's affection and respect. He was crazy about her!

Lillian's parents, my grandparents, Norman and Bessie Drucker, were from Vilnius, Lithuania. They came to the United States sharing hopes for a better life in a country they knew nothing about. Norman went ahead to secure a home for his family; he literally went out the back door with the Cossacks coming in the front. It was a narrow escape!

Bessie came after, traveling with their two young sons, without the benefit of knowing one word of English. She was terrified and spent much of the crossing on the ship's floor, clinging to her children and trusting her fate. She sat right next to the door and did not move during the entire trip. In Chicago, my grandparents added to their family with the births of their children George, Lillian, Sam, and Al. The Druckers were all hardworking and loyal to each other. In many ways, they were exemplary new Americans.

My mother's parents, Norman and Bessie Drucker, came to the United States from Lithuania.

My father's parents, Moses and Annie Elisberg, emigrated from Minsk, Belarus. They bought a grocery store on Chicago's northwest side, had eight children, and began to buy multiunit buildings for income property, when Moses died suddenly at the age of forty-two. Grandma Annie played the hand that life dealt her without complaint.

As a widow, she finished raising her children and continued to run the family's store, often offering credit when customers were short on cash. She was a strong woman involved in her community and her family. Her daughters inherited her pioneering spirit and drove cars (and got divorces) long before it was considered acceptable for ladies to exercise so much independence.

Moses Elisberg, my father's father, was a scholarly man. He died of a heart attack at forty-two.

My father left school in his teens to help his mother manage the store and the rental buildings; he never did graduate from high school. Eventually, Annie loaned him the capital to start a business on the condition that he make his brother Mike a business partner. Elisberg and Company quickly became a well-known and highly respected producer of quality women's coats. His factory was located on Franklin Street between Jackson and Van Buren, and at the height of his success, his was one of the top manufacturers in the Midwest.

By the time I was born, my dad was already making what was considered "good money" and was quite successful in his business. Yet, unconventionally, he was the one, not my mother, who walked the floor with me at night when I cried. Unlike my mother, or his mother, for that matter, my father knew how to express the tenderness in his heart. To my dad, it was natural to respond to a child's need for love and intimacy. But he understood that his place in the world was the office, not the nursery. So when my mother declared that tending to my every cry and complaint was unnecessary and would spoil me, my father put me back into my crib and retreated to the role that was ascribed to him by custom, culture, and his wife.

My father and I developed a close bond during my early childhood. In a time when men were not encouraged to stay home with their children, he was sensitive and caring.

My mother was by no means indifferent to the needs of her only child or unsympathetic to her husband's affectionate nature. After all, along with me, she herself was the recipient of his generosity of emotional spirit. Her way of looking at the world was quite different from his, but, still, they reconciled their similarities and formed a strong and respectful marriage. I always remember my father's simple but profound adoration of my mother. He withstood her periods of illness and cared for her both emotionally and physically.

It wasn't until the spring before my mother died—more than eight decades after I was born—that she acknowledged that she had missed something in life by not being able to engage more fully and admitted that she wished she had been able to express more warmth and intimacy in relationships. I wish that, too. But thinking back, it was from my father that I received my disposition: the gift of optimism, an affectionate nature, and the ability to engage and, when necessary, to disengage. From my mother, I received my intelligence, resilience, discipline, decorum, and style. The combination of qualities would come to serve me well in my life, and I am thankful for their gifts.

My mother was somewhat emotionally distant during my childhood, but she did the best she could to raise me in a loving and nurturing environment, with the help of my father.

The Vamp

After I was born, my mother suffered from what we now know as the rather serious condition of postpartum depression. Then, however, it was a nameless and often misdiagnosed "women's problem" that existed without much interference from the medical community. My mother's postnatal condition must have been exceptionally bad because her brother Sam attempted to give her a "sunshine cure" by taking her to Warner's Horse Ranch and Spa in Escondido, California. It obviously helped because my mother's depression, allergies, and fog of isolation that would continue to engulf her periodically throughout her life began to lift during her time there. She even made friends: a woman I remember as a frosty-tempered, massively obese British masseuse (perversely nicknamed Slim) and her handsome and overtly sensual French osteopath husband, Ben.

With all the fun in the sun, my mother's golden brown locks began to lighten, so as a special indulgence at the time (or to leave her imprint on my mother's looks), Slim bleached my mother's hair blond. Her transformation was drastic and exciting. The women in my mother's circle were all dark haired and heavyset; my mother stood out with her light hair and slim figure. My father always claimed that he loved her hair blond, and I honestly don't remember her any other way. To me, Mother was always beautiful, elegant, well dressed, and reserved—and blond.

Apparently, she was also uncharacteristically passionate about her new friends. Later, when I was almost two years old, my mother initiated a trip across the country to visit Ben and Slim at their home in Pasadena, California. My dad was a good sport, and we ventured west, where my mother's ailments once again drastically improved—so much so that she decided to extend her stay with her new friends.

My dad and I took the train back to Chicago without her. Grandma Bessie came to take care of me in my mother's absence. I was young yet remember the interlude fondly. Instead of missing Mother, I was thrilled with the attention and affection bestowed upon me by my grandmother. She gave me unconditional love and wrapped me in her warmth. She also tended to my educational development, once taking me to school and telling the principal, "I think she can go to school; she's very bright." She, too, had a high aptitude for learning and would later finally master English in her seventies when taking classes held by the WPA.

My grandfather Norman Drucker also spent time with me while my mother was away in California. This photo shows one of the first times I wore stockings, and I was very excited. My coat and my muff were made by father's coat business, Elisberg and Company.

When my mother returned from California, it didn't take long for her to become depressed again. The gray Chicago skies and stockyard-tainted air couldn't compete with gentle ocean breezes or her friends. California lured her back. She decided to return for the entire summer and this time to take me with her. Now I was the one who was unhappy.

Away from her new friends and fun times in California, my mother became depressed and distant. I sought her attention and felt rewarded when I received it.

In stark contrast to the care and companionship I had received from my Grandma Bessie, life in California with my mother during those months was a lonely and dark time for me. I could see that my mother's friends adored her. They called her "angel" and treated her with great affection. But their feelings about and treatment of me were confusing. They called me "the vamp," and Slim's husband paid attention to me in ways that I can describe only as creepy to a child (and possibly to any rational adult).

I remember feeling alone in an abject sense, ignored. Growing up as an only child, I had never felt such a sense of isolation, until then. There were no children to play with and no one to confide in. Even if I had had a larger vocabulary, I doubt I would have had the words to interpret my feelings at that time. I was just a child, alone among strangers, among them even my mother.

To fill my unmet emotional needs, I indulged in baked goods. Every day I walked along an expressway underpass to a little grocery store to buy myself a chocolate graham cracker or jelly-filled Bismarck. Going to get a treat was the highlight of each day, and no one ever seemed to notice my absence. I gained twenty-five pounds that summer.

Weight gain and loneliness weren't the worst of it. Being ignored by my mother and encountering Slim's distaste for me were nearly unbearable experiences, but I found the strange attention of Slim's seductive French husband worse. I had never encountered such a man—he was so unlike my kind and loving father or my other male relatives. Without the maturity to understand my discomfort, I spent the summer mired in unidentified feelings of isolation and unease. It was a very confusing time at a tender and impressionable age.

In a Bruno of Hollywood photo taken during this period, I see myself as a chubby child with a Clara Bow haircut and sad eyes. My tentative smile and self-aware expression seem both resigned and pleading. I was hardly what could be considered a "vamp." I was a little kid!

In this professional photo, circa Bruno Bernard, aka Bruno of Hollywood, a cute little girl was going through some difficult and confusing growing pains, brought on by a foreign environment and her mother's alienation.

Dance and Music

When we finally returned to Chicago, my mother registered me for dance lessons. Her high standards led me to study under Muriel Abbott, the premier dancing teacher in Chicago. To my mother, the arts were not about fun. They were about accomplishment, which, like everything else she introduced me to, would require discipline.

By way of an audition, I had to rehearse for and perform in the title role of a junior production of *Little Miss Muffet*. On opening night, like any first-time performer, my nerves nearly froze my little legs in place, and my mother had to literally push me onto the stage! I survived my trial and began studying dance and acrobatics under Mame Abbott's rigorous tutelage. The Muriel Abbott Dancers were nationally renowned for their youth, drive, and accomplishment, and I was proud to be among their ranks. To be trained by the immutable Muriel

Abbott and to eventually be invited to join this diva's stable of dancers were marks of distinction.

Studying dance and acrobatics under the direction of Muriel Abbott prepared me to perform throughout my life. I loved my time on the stage!

My mother was a great believer not just in doing your best but also in being the best. She and Ms. Abbott were identical in their orientations, and I wanted nothing more than to live up to their expectations. However, at the same time, despite my quest for perfection, I really began to love performing and found my time on the stage to be as exciting as it was fulfilling.

The dancing came quite naturally, but the acrobatics training scared me so much that only my desire to succeed made me continue. Away from the studio, I practiced walking on my hands down my mother's very long hallway, and I used a mattress to practice the aerials. In short time, my hard work helped me to develop a masterful style. By then I had learned that with practice and patience, I could do whatever I set my mind to.

My mother was a good stage mother. I worked to gain her approval and her attention, and she responded by being entirely accommodating and encouraging. Always the prettiest mother in the group and beautifully dressed, she sat in the audience for every practice and, later, most performances. She cheered me on in her quiet way, and it was fully rewarding. First through dance—and later myriad other accomplishments—I learned how to hold her interest and garner her support.

When I was eight years old—a dancing veteran—it was decided that I should add to my repertoire with music lessons. Again, my mother turned to a European master. Josef Kindl was Czechoslovakian. He graduated from the Prague Conservatory and was a former professor at Charles University. He studied with Franz Liszt before immigrating to the United States and demonstrated the Old World orientation and ethic that my mother must have shared on some level. For years, I practiced piano for two to five hours a day. I was playing Beethoven before my feet comfortably reached the pedals!

Dr. Kindl was strict. His command of English was insufficient and his passion overpowering; out of sheer excitement, he once pushed me so hard that I fell off the piano bench! Watchful but unworried, Mother quietly rectified the problem the first time it happened by purchasing an antique piano bench with a carved back for my safety. Thus, I stayed in my seat, and Kindl-style discipline stayed in my life.

Talented, rigid, and temperamental, Kindl was to music what Abbott was to dance and Lillian was to mothering. They all had rules and made sure I abided by them. I did not rebel; I was determined to meet whatever bar was set for me and worked cheerfully to please the demands of my three masters. As I look back, I see my mother's style of mothering as exacting and encouraging as might be expected from someone who had one standard of excellence: the best. She accepted nothing less than my highest efforts and impeccable behavior. Once, I took a piece of gum off the kitchen table without asking and ended up in the closet to think about my crime.

Although the discipline, demands, and expectations of my early childhood may seem extreme now, they would all prove to be good training for meeting life's challenges and overcoming difficulties. I learned the value of hard work and determination, and I believe my unwillingness to fail took root around this time.

Hyde Park History

In the months before the stock market crashed, my family moved into a spacious apartment on the third floor of a three-floor red brick building at 5529 Hyde Park Boulevard. The South Side community was safe and friendly, nestled among beautiful mansions and the prestigious University of Chicago. I had my own room, with a twin bed with a white pom-pom bedspread, a dresser, and a small closet. Best of all for an only child, there were five sisters living just two floors down. My first childhood romance was also cultivated in that building with a cute young blond named Wilson Button (who would, much later in life, become senior vice president of Sears in Chicago).

I went to school in the neighborhood, starting at Bret Harte for a brief stint and continuing at Kenwood (later Kenwood Academy) and Hyde Park High School. The schools were all quite a distance from our home, so my dad drove me there every day in his Buick.

Shortly after we moved in to our new apartment, we had an unexpected houseguest. Mother's brother Sam had a fire in his own apartment and moved into the extra room off our kitchen. We thought he was coming for a short time, but he ended up staying for twelve years! Uncle Sam was a good-looking fellow who resembled the actor Dick Van Dyke. After graduating from Columbia University—the first Drucker to earn a degree—he developed a successful greeting card line that he eventually sold so he could join his brother George in the photography business. During the twelve years that Sam lived with us, he spent his days working as a chemical engineer with his brother and his evenings happily ensconced at our home with us.

My mother's brother Sam lived with my family for nearly twelve years while I was growing up. I enjoyed having my uncle around, and we had fun together over the years.

When the stock market crashed, thankfully, we didn't feel it to the degree that so many others did. Yet, compared with the very wealthy families of some of the other girls I knew who went to private school and wore furs, our family had different hardships. Mother had to cancel some furniture and china she had ordered for our new apartment, and she chose her groceries a bit more carefully, but we continued to have a maid who came in to help with the house and even a telephone in the hallway (though it was a pay phone). Later in life I became aware that my father had lost a good deal of money in the stock market, but during the time, I don't ever remember feeling that we suffered. We had what we had, and we were all right.

Two months after the crash, with nearly half of Chicago out of work, I was lucky enough to go to work for what was then the handsome sum of $45 per week. I was eleven years old, and after my success in her classes, I had been invited to become a dancer in Muriel Abbott's Professional Revue. Over Christmas break, the troupe, composed of eleven- to thirteen-year-old budding Rockettes, was hired to do three live shows a day as intermission entertainment between movies at theaters ranging from the Chicago Theatre downtown, to the Tivoli Theatre in the Woodlawn neighborhood south of the city, to the Marlboro and Granada theaters on the North Side.

As a dancer in Muriel Abbott's Professional Revue, I was among a group of budding Rockettes. We learned the power of performance and perseverance—the show had to go on at all costs! (I am shown at the far left.)

Our job as tap dancers and acrobats was to distract people from their fears and pains with a smile and a dance. Building on my beginnings with Mame Abbott, I continued what I think was probably the best education of my life. It became clearer and clearer to me that the show must go on, no matter what.

During my professional stage experience, a series of mishaps taught me how to handle nearly any situation. I learned the value of improvisation. Once, as if out of one of the movies at the theater, someone in the audience threw a banana peel on stage. I slipped on it but got right back up and kept performing, hardly missing a beat.

Because of my gracefulness and poise, I was given the duty of leading all the other dancers off the stage at the end of the performance. There were two exits, the path to one much longer than that to the other, and the song Ms. Abbott had chosen for our departure was too short for the long exit—and I told her as much. Just as I knew would happen, by the time everyone had made the exit she insisted we take, the music had stopped. Ms. Abbott was fuming, and she shook me violently as I came off the stage—but then gave me a taffy apple to apologize. She had a very strong temper.

On New Year's Eve 1929, the entire production was arrested for violating child labor laws because we were up past our bedtimes and performing as the clock struck midnight. The other young dancers and I were detained by police for an hour and a half and then released. We couldn't believe it—and neither could our parents—but it was part of the fun. I loved it all and wanted to go on dancing forever.

A Dream Deferred

By the time I was a freshman at Hyde Park High School, the Abbott Dancers had moved into Chicago's prestigious Empire Room in the beautiful Palmer House Hotel. Young women now, we were local celebrities, as the troupe was gaining both a national and international reputation. The older girls in the group were even taken to South America.

Suddenly, out of the blue, my father told me that my career on the stage was over. "That's it" were the exact words he used. He explained that he didn't mind my dancing as a child but felt that it wasn't right for a young lady. Because of his experience in the clothing business, he had worked with models and knew more about the seedy underbelly of show business than I did. He was concerned for my safety and my future. I had no choice but to obey his wishes. Unfortunately, in those days, you believed what your father said and did what he told you to do.

I was disappointed and had hoped that my mother would intervene. After all, she was the one who had incited, supported, and promoted my desires to be on the stage from the time I was a little girl. Yet, as she watched her daughter being denied her dreams, she didn't intercede on my behalf. Like me, she went along with my father's decisions.

Even now, one of my biggest regrets in life is that I wasn't able to pursue a career in entertainment. I loved being on stage, and the stage loved me. To this day, I still fondly remember it as one of the happiest and best times in my life. I believe I had a real talent and wish I could have taken it further. At the time, however, I simply and obediently (if reluctantly) switched gears and began to pursue interests that were considered more appropriate for a young lady, namely, fund-raising and dieting, both of which would require the self-determination and discipline that I had learned in the pursuit of my first passion.

Womanly Pursuits

Fund-raising and dieting came to me in a serious way on the same day, at a charity luncheon during Christmas break of my sophomore year in 1933. Before that time, I hadn't given either subject much thought. When I had tickets to school sporting events or performances to sell, I sold them. I had a job to do, and I did it, and like other things, I found that I was very good at it. I came by it honestly, I suppose: my father had done the same as president of the garment union when it was necessary to raise money for various things. His mother was similar.

In fact, Grandma Annie literally refused to lie down and die the year she was eighty-seven until she had finished the charity work she had committed to.

At that particular luncheon, a heavyset girl and her mother were seated with my mother and me at the same table. When the girl took a second éclair for dessert, a premonition flashed before my eyes, and I saw myself destined for chubbiness. Despite all the dancing and acrobatics throughout my girlhood, I had somehow remained plump. For some reason, it never really bothered me until that day at the luncheon when I came face-to-face with what very well could have been my future. I asked my mother to help me diet, and she said she would.

From that day on everything I ate was cut in half. I eliminated desserts and ate lots of apples. At an age when most girls begin to pack on estrogen-induced pounds, I took them off. By June, I had lost thirty-two pounds. I looked and felt like a new person. My newfound confidence helped me raise money for a variety of school activities, and in the process I gained more valuable skills, contacts, and visibility as I emerged from the protective camouflage of "baby fat" and into plain sight. Seemingly miraculously and overnight, I had developed into a stunning young lady.

In this photo from my confirmation, my thirty-two-pound weight loss revealed a pretty young lady developing self-confidence, style, and charm (center).

With the loss of all that weight, I gained a lot of male attention. My social group was a mixture of South and North Shore residents, and there were lots of parties and open houses at various homes. We had fun! It was a whirlwind, but we were safe and innocent, protected by the mores of the time. Some kids were drinking and smoking—but not me. I knew the consequences. When I was thirteen, I once endured a four-day silent treatment from my mother when I told her I had tried a cigarette. I wasn't a Goody Two-shoes, but I didn't want to go through that again!

More important than the idle frolicking and social experimentation, we teens were learning how to navigate through society and accept its realities. There were times when I would have liked to have had certain things but my mother said no. When I started wearing more dresses as a young woman, my mother agreed to buy me a few inexpensive ones but only one good gown. She ingrained in me the idea of quality over quantity. I wore my best dress, a red silk sheath, over and over and didn't care about the repeats because I knew it looked nice. No one ever seemed to notice, and I always looked—and felt—fabulous.

At the first party I ever attended, not knowing what else to do, I stood in one place the whole evening and eventually found myself inundated with male attention. Soon enough, I had so many dates that guys would wait weeks for their turn to take me out. I was so naive I thought it was the same for everybody; little did I know how lucky I was! I was carefree and fell in and out of love all the time.

Bud Simon was one of the boys I met during this exciting time. A year my senior, he was a wavy-haired blond sixteen-year-old from Glencoe with a smile that lit my heart. The night I met him, I remember telling my mother that I had met "the cleanest boy I've ever seen."

I liked him immediately, and he seemed to fall in love with me that night. We were too young to commit to a serious relationship but continued to develop a deep and binding friendship. Bud had his own car when we met and would happily drive the thirty miles from his home in Glencoe to mine in Hyde Park. The blond young man and the blossoming young girl were both filled with possibility—for ourselves as well as the world that seemed to revolve around us. We were young, dancing and dreaming and meeting each other's families with the confidence of kids ready to take on the world. Bud's father offered me a house that first summer if I married his son. Stunned, I just laughed. What's a house to a fifteen-year-old?

A Model Student

High school was a great time. My school pictures reveal a petite girl wearing lovely clothes and a big white-toothed smile. I was active in the Freshie Frolic Committee, Booster Club, French Honor Society, and Welfare Committee of student government. In my junior year, I was elected treasurer and president of the Junior Girls' Club, member of the Election Committee, editor of the annual yearbook, and coordinator of division room pictures. Also, while only boys were eligible to be president of our graduating class, I was elected to the highest post my gender would allow—vice president of the June '35 graduating class.

As a budding young woman in high school, I was active in many extracurricular activities such as the Booster Club and the French Honor Society. It was a wonderful time full of fun and friends.

I was so lucky. We all were. It was an easy and protected time in our lives. No one was afraid of anything. Life was a pleasure socially, and I was always willing to take responsibility and be a leader. High school was like my own personal Camelot.

The summer before my senior year in high school, I worked at Burke and James, a photo supply company owned by Mother's brothers in downtown Chicago. My responsibilities were mostly filing, but when I wasn't shuffling papers, I sat for photographs that my uncles used for ads. I was selected for a prominent Pepsodent toothpaste ad because of my sweet smile.

High school was a wonderful time—my personal Camelot.

My uncles were very strict. There were limited lunchtimes, no breaks, and no goofing off. Still, I managed to enjoy myself. Working for them taught me to pay attention to everything, even what I saw as the "boring" secretarial aspects of the job. I was rewarded for my diligence when my uncles doubled my salary at the end of a few weeks.

The University of Chicago

I was only just seventeen when I started at the University of Chicago, because I had been put ahead in grammar school. Although I wanted to go east, my parents insisted that I live at home and attend the University of Chicago because it was $100 per quarter and the country remained in the grips of the Depression. Though not deeply affected, my parents were still being cautious. I was disappointed but knew the U of C was a reputable school and accepted my fate.

Worse, however, than not getting to go where I wanted to go, I wasn't able to study what I wanted to study. This time it was my mother who pulled the rug out from under me. I had always had a deep desire to make a difference, to make things better, so I decided on social work as a major. However, my mother convinced me that it was an inappropriate area of study for me because she thought I was physically too small for the dangers that social workers often come into contact with. She said I should take classes in education instead. I never wanted to be a teacher, but the coursework ended up serving me well in my life.

Upon beginning my collegiate career, the most difficult situation for me was that after being an honor student my whole life, I was denied an academic scholarship. Suddenly, I felt intimidated and second-guessed my abilities. While I can pinpoint the invasion of insecurity to the moment I received the news of my rejection by the scholarship committee, the feeling never quite went away completely.

The second humbling experience was my introduction to anti-Semitism. Thankfully, I had largely managed to avoid it up to that point in my life because throughout high school, there were so many other Jewish kids (as well as several black students) it made for a good balance. I never once felt singled out or out of place for my Jewish heritage.

In college, however, I experienced for the first time things being denied to me on the basis of my background. Although it was extremely subtle and largely unspoken, Jews were excluded from the girls' social clubs. I accepted the discrimination as simply "the way it was" but was never unconscious of the fact that "it shouldn't be." The girls who had to bar me from their clubs were otherwise nice girls who also accepted my exclusion as status quo. We were all raised well and didn't question, let alone challenge, the customs handed down to us. In fact, some of those girls were even my good friends. I sat on boards with many of them, including, ironically, the Women's Board of the University of Chicago, where I took an active role in planning university activities.

As a college student, I continued to be willing to assume risk and responsibility, as I had in my teenage years, always taking on more than I had to. But the incongruity of working so hard for people who had rules in place to exclude me, based on my religion, was never unrecognized. In practice, I hid whatever personal and academic insecurity I had beneath a veil of straight As and did my best to ignore the ignorance and damage of prejudice, institutional or otherwise. Perhaps today I am more sensitive and empathetic toward others as a result of this experience.

PART II

Back to California

Before the start of my junior year, little did I know but my dream of being a star would be reignited on another visit to California with Mother. We were staying at the lovely Langham Hotel in Hollywood. While Mother visited with her old friends Slim and Ben, I was old enough to opt out of the reunion and made my own new friends. I met a wonderful young man at the hotel pool who was on vacation from Austin, Texas. He was tall and handsome and already looked like a movie star. His name also happened to be Marion, and it didn't take long before we began a summer romance that included seeing the sights together.

One day we went for sodas at Schwab's Pharmacy, located at 8024 Sunset Boulevard. Hollywood legend holds that in 1936, Lana Turner was "discovered" sitting on a fountain stool at Schwab's. I don't know about her, but I do know that I was approached by Hollywood scouts there that very same year. Marion and I were blissfully unaware that at the time, Schwab's was the place for actors and wannabes, deal makers and deal takers. Insiders referred to it as "headquarters." We just wanted some chocolate sodas!

Sometime before Marion and I finished our drinks, a gal came up to us and asked whether we were interested in the movies. To put it mildly, we were! Before we knew it, we were each invited to meet the famous producer Joseph Schenck on the studio lot of Twentieth Century Fox. Schenck would end up playing a key role in the development of the film industry, but we, of course, didn't know that then. All I knew was that despite my father's desire to keep me out of the entertainment business, fate kept reeling me back in.

The day I walked into Mr. Schenck's office, he was already a powerful man: the first president of United Artists and a partner in Twentieth Century Pictures, among other accolades. Unaware of his résumé and unintimidated by his prestige, I was almost completely focused on what I perceived to be my glaring flaw: chubby legs. In a clumsy effort at concealment, I stood behind the chair he offered me to sit in. To his credit, he allowed me to do so without comment. After a few minutes of conversation, he told me that I didn't need a screen test and handed me a contract. He told me to sign it and send it back.

I was beside myself with joy, but it didn't last. When I told my father, he said, "Absolutely not." Mother concurred. I obeyed. Disappointed but not bitter, upset but not rebellious, I respected my parents' wishes because I had been raised to do what I was told and at that point I was still doing it. Once again, I said, "OK."

I was offered a film contract with Twentieth Century Fox, but my parents did not approve. This was a photo I gave to the studio as my "promotional" shot; I think it helped me land the deal!

My friend Marion received the same contract offer from Mr. Schenck, which he immediately signed and returned. I was happy for him and spent the rest of the summer helping him get rid of his Texas accent. Eventually, he changed his name from Marion Goodman to Don Castle and was cast in the Andy Hardy movies with Mickey Rooney and Judy Garland. He wrote me long, beautiful letters for years about his life first in movies and later in real estate.

For years, every time I saw Judy Garland, I wished I could have had a chance. I wondered how far I might have gone. I wanted to try musical comedy so badly; I just know it would have been a lot of fun. Instead, I went back to the University of Chicago to finish my degree in a major not of my own choosing.

Don Castle was my summer romance during yet another trip to California with my mother. He appeared in many movies and television shows.

Betty Co-Ed

In my junior year, much to my surprise yet building on my close brush with stardom, my friends nominated me for the University of Chicago's version of a homecoming queen, called Betty Co-Ed. I had probably always taken my looks for granted, but I was thrilled to be thought of in that way. For some reason unbeknownst to me, the boys in the three main fraternities stuffed the ballot boxes all over campus with my name. I won.

MIDWAY QUEEN

She is Marion Elisberg, 19, and she was selected Friday by student vote to be Homecoming Queen at the football game between the University of Chicago and Ohio State on Saturday. She was chosen from a field of eleven.

In my college years, I won a campus beauty contest and was elected Betty Co-Ed and homecoming queen. This photo ran in the evening newspaper.

I was Betty Co-Ed homecoming queen for the Ohio State game and quickly forgot about the disappointments in California in the rush of excitement. An anonymous admirer sent me flowers. Radio stations interviewed me. In an elegant and exciting celebration at Don Roth's Blackhawk Restaurant on Wabash, I was presented with a trophy by the famous bandleader Kay Kyser. My date was a really handsome boy by the name of Bob Greenebaum. Bob, a shy football player, became my college sweetheart, and at one point, we almost ran away to get married.

My date to the Betty Co-Ed coronation was Bob Greenebaum, who later became my college romance. We were introduced by his mother, who was taking classes at the University of Chicago. He and I shared many experiences together, including once being robbed on the Congress Street Bridge!

One particularly memorable experience during our time together was when we were robbed on the Congress Street Bridge! We had gone to see Benny Goodman play at the Congress Hotel. After the show, Bob and I were necking in his father's car, parked on the bridge, when a man opened the door and got in. He pointed a gun at us and told us to give him our money and our car. We were instructed to get out and wait on Columbus Drive for twenty minutes. Bob gave him the $15 he had in his wallet, and we stood outside in the freezing cold (twenty-two degrees below zero!). We couldn't believe what was happening, and all I could think about was how worried my mother would be. To our surprise, the thief actually came back and left the car in front of the Auditorium Building, just as he promised us he would!

After our harrowing experience, Bob and I continued to see each other. However, as many romances do during those flirtatious formative years, it did not last; we parted at the beginning of our senior year.

When famous bandleader Kay Kyser (left) and Paul Fogarty (right), who wrote the popular song "Betty Co-Ed," presented me with my trophy for homecoming queen at Don Roth's Blackhawk, I was over the moon!

The most memorable moments of my Betty Co-Ed coronation occurred during the game's halftime, when I was called onto the field. I looked at the excitement of the crowd, felt the sunshine, and heard the thunder of applause. I was on the stage once again.

My exposure as Betty Co-Ed brought the attention of many friends and their families alike. An eclectic father of a good friend, Katherine Freund, must have been impressed by the acclaim of my title, and he invited me to join them on a four-week trip to Jamaica. Surprisingly, Mother agreed to let me go—but only after the dean of the university wholeheartedly supported the endeavor and consented to let me continue my studies in the Caribbean.

It was fantastic. To be on the Panama Clipper flying over the ocean was exciting beyond belief. Once we got to Jamaica, it was another world. The heat. The colors. The smells. The tastes. Everything was new to us. Katherine and I had to figure out how to wash our hair with china spittoons. Every morning, we would study in what we called our "little lizard bawdy house" because lizards were procreating everywhere in the heat, humidity, and greenery.

To see the hallowed "Blue Mountain sunrise," we climbed the famous range in the rain—oh, the rain! Our journey, on the backs of donkeys, started at 1 a.m. in a dreadful downpour that didn't let up for seven hours. During the trek, as I tried to keep my hands dry in the pockets of my pitifully short coat, I found a note my mother had written to the dry-cleaners to be sure they removed a stain. I had to chuckle to myself. If only they—and she—could see me now! Finally, when we made it to the top, we huddled under a small piece of tin to escape the deluge and sipped hot coffee and tea to revive our soggy bones. Only when we began our retreat down the mountain did the skies clear. We were treated to the remarkably beautiful sight of the sun rising up out of the ocean. At the end of the pass, a local woman greeted us with armfuls of tiny exotic orchids.

During the rest of our vacation, we walked through seemingly endless miles of ferns, toured the entire island, and stopped in the Florida Everglades on the way back. At the end I marveled at the wonderful experience. I came back a changed woman—worldlier and a bit wiser.

Adventures in Romance

Once back in Chicago, I got a call from a friend, Eddie Goodkind, who said there was a fellow in town from Dartmouth whom he thought I should meet. His name was Alan Tishman. He was handsome and charming, the grandson of real estate magnate Julius Tishman. When I first saw him, all I could think was "Wow!" He was very good looking.

Alan was in town for only three days, but I fell for him right away, and we spent every waking moment together. He was very tall, very smart, very considerate—and did I mention very handsome?

This handsome fellow is Alan Tishman, whom I had a relationship with during my college years. We remained good friends throughout our lives.

He was also very wealthy. So wealthy that instead of thinking my family was privileged to have a telephone during the Depression, or even just taking it for granted as I did, he was amazed that it was in the hallway and actually needed coins. Despite our families' financial differences, we had a great time dancing and talking and just being together. We became very close in a short time, and he invited me to his family's house in New York for Thanksgiving.

Once again, to my surprise, my mother agreed to let me go. I took the Twentieth Century Limited, an express passenger train that traveled between Grand Central Terminal in New York City and LaSalle Street Station in Chicago. Intended for the upper class, as well as business travelers, the Twentieth Century boasted sleeping compartments and an elegant dining car and routinely made the 938-mile journey in only fifteen and one-half hours. Best of all, when passengers walked to and from the train at either station, a plush crimson carpet was rolled out for them to walk upon—thus originating the concept of "red-carpet treatment."

It was all so dramatic. Everyone was well dressed, and the train itself was gorgeous. I felt very grown-up. I was taking the Twentieth Century Limited by myself to meet my boyfriend for a holiday! This after just having taken the Panama Clipper to Jamaica! I was so wound up by the time I got off the train and walked across the red carpet toward a very handsome 6'2" man I could barely think. My head was spinning!

Thanksgiving dinner was at the Tishmans' gorgeous Park Avenue apartment. It was as if *Town and Country* magazine had come to life as a Noël Coward play featuring beautiful people in amazing clothing who displayed impeccable manners. It was all very nice, and Alan's mother was especially charming and took to me right away.

At night Alan and I went dancing in Manhattan. He showed me a wonderful time. As we toured the Big Apple, my eyes boggled a bit every time I saw a bus pass by with a sign plastered on its side advertising Tishman Realty. Because I didn't want to be presumptuous and stay with Alan's family while I was visiting, I stayed with my childhood friend Adele Bretzfield in her dorm at Columbia University. We were close and had even been confirmed together, in the days before bat mitzvahs. Long after she would eventually marry Willard Gidwitz, the president of Helene Curtis Industries, we stayed close confidantes.

Tish and I had a sweet relationship, but it wasn't a crazy thing. I didn't go to bed with him if that's what you're wondering. You never went to bed with anybody back then. You were either "a girl who did" or "a girl who didn't," and I didn't. By taking the sexual experience out of these kinds of budding relationships, you really got to know each other without the blur of sensuality that tends to skew one's thinking.

Though I was trying to keep things simple when it came to my romantic endeavors, my "boy trouble" was about to begin. By sheer coincidence, Bud Simon also happened to be in New York for the Thanksgiving weekend, and he wanted to see me. Somehow I managed both guys by spending early dates with one and late dates with another. I knew that I loved Alan but at the time was not sure how I felt about Bud. However, I had fun with both men, and it was certainly a busy and exciting trip! I loved New York. Little did I know how soon I would return.

Bud Simon and I met in high school, and he would continue to be a constant in my life.

New York World's Fair

The Elgin Watch Company was holding a competition to discover the most beautiful and brightest American college girls to represent it and the state of Illinois as greeters at the 1939 World's Fair in New York the following summer. The young women would be selected from among thousands of co-eds at Big Ten universities for their personality, beauty, grace, character, and scholastic standing.

At the University of Chicago, whoever won the top honor for a senior girl, Head Score Girl for the Blackfriar's Club, also won the opportunity to act as the University of Chicago representative in Elgin's "Big Ten of Beauty" at the New York World's Fair. The winner would be selected by Bob Crosby, Bing's brother, at an event held—once again—at the popular and swanky Blackhawk Restaurant. Entrants were eventually reduced to twelve finalists, ten with club affiliations (groups from which I was banned) and two independents, one of which was me. Although I was a finalist nominated by both the faculty and my peers, my parents were unenthusiastic about my chances.

"Forget it," they both said. They didn't think I could compete with the other girls. Defeated and disappointed in my parents' lack of support, I reluctantly agreed not to go to the affair.

Then I snapped out of it. This time, my dutiful daughter personality became engaged in a mighty fight with my welling desire for the stage and the independence I'd consistently been denied. I would not let my dream die.

The night of the selection, I was at an engagement party that ended early. On a whim I asked my date, Jack Mackintosh, to go with me to the Blackhawk. Even though I doubted my chances, I thought it would be fun to see the hubbub. When he agreed to accompany me, I was emboldened and promised the entire engagement party that if I won, I would treat everyone to champagne at the Blackhawk—but nobody came! Turns out I wasn't the only one with doubts.

Walking into the Blackhawk that night was like déjà vu. It had been only a year since Kay Kyser had presented me with a trophy on the very same stage for winning the title of Betty Co-Ed. I had goose bumps, but I wasn't nervous because I honestly didn't think I would win.

The eleven other girls were dressed to the nines, but I wore a simple navy dress with a white collar, my outfit from the engagement party. When it was my turn to go to the middle of the dance floor to be interviewed, I was so excited and caught up in the moment I could never tell you what I said! The singer Marian Mann kept winking at me. "Are you part of this?" she asked. I said, "I could be," and she responded by saying, "Well, get over here, then!" The next thing I knew, the lights were shining on me, and I was holding three dozen American Beauty roses as I was awarded the Head Score Girl for the Blackfriar Productions. I was given a paid job for five weeks at the New York World's Fair Elgin concession, all expenses paid!

I would be featured on national radio programs, presented to the mayor of New York and fair officials, and shown the sights of the city while photographers snapped my picture. It was so unreal that even my parents didn't believe I had won until they saw a headline in the morning paper that read: "Independent Marion Elisberg Wins."

U. of C. Winner

[TRIBUNE Photo.]

MARION ELISBERG.

Miss Marion Elisberg, 5529 Hyde Park boulevard, will be head musical score girl for the annual Blackfriars show at the University of Chicago April 21, 22, 28, and 29. She was selected Friday night by Bob Crosby, orchestra leader, and two other judges, from ten co-eds contesting for the honor. Miss Elisberg is 20 years old and a senior. She will be awarded a month's trip to the New York fair by a watch company.

In my senior year of college, seemingly against all odds, I was voted Head Score Girl for the Blackfriar's Club and whisked away to the New York World's Fair in 1939, courtesy of the Elgin Watch Company. My family and friends didn't believe my good fortune—literally—until they saw it for themselves in the paper!

All I had to do to was pass my comprehensive senior exams. Although I earned A grades, I remained shaken by not having received an academic scholarship and nervous about being tested and not measuring up. I always wanted to do my best and not fail. Despite my terrors, I passed!

However, there was no time to celebrate. Before embarking on my new adventure in New York at the World's Fair, I spent my last months at the University of Chicago in an exciting whirlwind: meeting politicians, staying as a guest at the Congress Hotel, going to nightclubs, and being photographed at a series of events sponsored by the ad agency J. W. Thompson. My favorite was a cow-milking contest held on the campus Midway. To promote the upcoming Blackfriar production, a play called *Butter and Egg Man*, two of the actors "milked" the publicity for all it was worth, literally. The winner, Lew Hamity, a U of C fullback who later played for the Chicago Bears, won the honor of escorting me to the play. Being a beauty queen definitely had its perks!

But with all of the doors opening (and cameras clicking) in front of me, a very significant door was closing. Just before graduation, my flames Alan Tishman and Bud Simon both returned to Chicago to "talk." Alan said that he was really sorry but "committed" to a girl named Peggy Westheimer from Wellesley. He said he had been dating her before he met me and had recently decided that she was going be "it" for him. It felt like a punch in the gut, but I was pretty good about it. I assumed that I couldn't fight it since I lived out of town, and I decided to give up gracefully. Then, on the same day that Tish told me I wasn't his heart's desire, Bud insisted that I meet him for lunch at the drug store on 55th Street and Everett, where he announced that if I didn't marry him, it was going to be over between us.

It was so odd. The day one man tells me it isn't going to be me, another one insists that it is going to be me. I was overwhelmed. As I tried to process it all, I realized that I had been in and out of love over the years, but Bud was there through all of it. I appreciated our relationship, but I wasn't excited about it. I thought of him as a friend—a good friend. Finally realizing I just wasn't ready, I broke the news to Bud. He was upset but held out hope; he gave me a dime-store ring, saying, "I'll give you a real one whenever you say the word."

In the midst of my matters of the heart, in June of 1939, I graduated from the University of Chicago with a bachelor's degree in English. I had lost one man of my dreams and had another man waiting for me. I was only twenty years old and ready to take New York by storm, compliments of the Elgin Watch Company. To ease us into our World's Fair experience in style—and create as many photo opportunities as possible—Elgin treated the "Big Ten" girls to one week of living at the Ritz-Carlton and sightseeing.

Another milestone preceded my departure for New York and the World's Fair—graduation! I handily passed my comprehensive senior exams and, at age twenty, received my bachelor's in English. I'll never forget walking down the long aisle at Rockefeller Chapel with the rest of my class.

I barely remember the train ride to New York, but I'll never forget walking into the Ritz for the first time and seeing—of all people—Alan Tishman in the lobby waiting for me! It had been a few months since our sad conversation, but there he was. He was talking on the lobby telephone. Did we kiss? Did we embrace, as if out of a movie? I don't remember. I do remember him being thrilled to see me, wanting to introduce me to some of his friends. His smile was wide and genuine, but there was a lack of an explanation for his being there. I assumed that he had read about my arrival in the paper, but I have no idea how he knew exactly when I was coming.

Despite my resigned disappointment that he had chosen Peggy over me, I responded to his casual affection and offer of friendship. Our connection would turn out to be as powerful as it was platonic. We solidified our lifelong friendship. But, as it turns out, after being the one to break my heart, he introduced me to my next semiserious romance.

Orvil Dryfoos was a smooth and well-bred gentleman. Handsome and educated, he was everything a girl could want—aside from being Alan Tishman. He had a seat on the New York Stock Exchange at the time and was a lovely man. Over the summer, we went everywhere together, and he showed me a wonderful time. He drove a red convertible, and when a friend's mother saw me driving around downtown New York with the top down, having the time of my life, word got around about my thrilling experiences.

During our week at the Ritz, the Elgin Watch Company treated us like movie stars. They had Schiaparelli design celestial uniform dresses reminding people that time was once told by looking at the sky. The frocks were cut from blue silk dotted with tiny star constellations. We were wined and dined and placed in the public eye throughout Manhattan with the heady pleasure of cameras following us.

BOSTON TRAVELER, MONDAY, JULY 24, 1939

(Wide World Photo)

PRETTY HOSTESSES from mid-western colleges, who will be seen in the Elgin time observatory at the New York World's Fair. The girls, shown on arrival at Grand Central station, are, left to right, Frances H. Goodwin of Ohio State, Marcia Connell of Michigan, Marion Elisberg of Chicago, Adelaide Salmon of Minnesota, Joyce B. Francke of Wisconsin. Rear, Libby Rice of Indiana, Treva Berry of Purdue, Rosemary Best of Illinois, Edith Prior-Leahy of Iowa and Sally Douglas of Northwestern.

The "Big Ten of Beauty" girls and I were treated like celebrities during our stint in New York at the World's Fair. It was a marvelous time, and we experienced all that the city had to offer when we weren't working at the fair.

After the first thrilling week, Elgin provided all of us with an apartment near the World's Fair in Flushing. Mother, however, would not agree to that option for me. She loved New York and came as my chaperone to secure a simple apartment for us on 44th Street and Second Avenue. I took a shuttle daily to Rockefeller Center and a subway to the fair, but I hardly minded any minor inconvenience of the commute. Life was so thrilling. I was living in the heart of the city, not out in a suburb like the rest of the girls.

During my time at the World's Fair, my mother didn't want to miss out on the fun; she came to join me, and we lived together in an apartment downtown.

The New York World's Fair was monumentally exciting, but it wasn't my first experience with such an epic event. I had been to the 1933 Chicago World's Fair, where, at the Kodak Building, my uncle George demonstrated the camera flashbulb and photo enlarger he had invented. In the Hall of Science, I saw fascinating new things, such as a figure showing the inside of a human body, including all the veins and arteries, and human embryos in various stages. I loved the science displays and, at fifteen, posed as a twelve-year-old so I could get in for a nickel. Every day for one week straight, I went to the hall to explore all the new and unusual things.

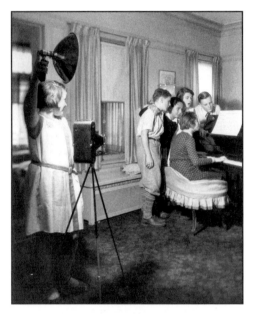

The New York World's Fair wasn't my first. When I was a girl, I was part of the 1933 World's Fair in Chicago and helped my uncle showcase his photographic inventions.

Also at the Chicago World's Fair, I spent many days marveling at the unusual new discoveries in the Hall of Science.

At the New York fair, the General Motors Building and General Electric Building were filled with college students, in addition to visitors from around the world. I never tired of explaining the history of various clocks on display inside of bell jars or just talking and connecting with the seemingly endless stream of people who came to our exhibit.

At the New York World's Fair, the Elgin Watch Company's clocks and watches were showcased. It was our duty as Elgin girls to explain everything to the visitors streaming in and out of our exhibit.

The Elgin Watch Company's artifacts were displayed in bell jars, and visitors from around the world came to the World's Fair to learn about their inner workings. I never tired of discussing the details or interacting with all the wonderful people.

My hours were fabulous. My shift was from noon to 8 p.m., so I didn't have to rush in the morning. I came home on the 8:28 subway, and by 9:45, I was out again at the Stork Club or the 21 Club having fun with Orvil and the rest of my friends. We took advantage of everything Manhattan had to offer, literally skipping down the street arm in arm singing "We're off to see the wizard," in giddy imitation of Dorothy and her fellow seekers after we had seen *The Wizard of Oz* on the silver screen.

One day at the fair I got a visitor who was more interested in me than clocks or bell jars. I was explaining the history of a timepiece when I noticed a tall, dark-haired girl looking me over. I don't know how, but I knew who she was. I asked her, "Are you Peggy Westheimer?" I thought she would die! I understood Alan's fiancée's impulse to check me out. I was as curious about her as she was about me, and we had a short but pleasant conversation, during which, like two well-mannered rivals, we sized each other up. Interestingly, Mother and I actually ended up having lunch with Peggy, Alan, and Orvil before she and I returned to Chicago. We were all on our best behavior, and it was a nice way to finish the summer.

And what an amazing summer it had been! A lovely romance, a salaried job, and memories for a lifetime. For my service, I received a watch from the Elgin Watch Company that still keeps time nearly five decades later.

During my summer in New York at the fair, I received a stipend of $25 a week for my service—quite a large amount of money at that time!

ELGIN NATIONAL WATCH COMPANY

NEW YORK WORLD'S FAIR

Employee   MARION E. ELISBERG

Social Security Number

Week ending   Aug. 4, 1939

Wages payable $ 25.20

Deductions:

Social Security $ .25

Amount of Check $ 24.95

Building on my experience and exposure at the New York World's Fair, I represented the state of Illinois in publicity material.

Stalled Mergers

After my amazing experiences being in front of so many people in New York, I made inquiries about the possibility of modeling in Chicago. A representative from the Powers modeling agency told me to forget it, in a polite but indifferent way. I looked nothing like the models of the day, but I thought I at least had a chance based on my previous experience with Betty Co-Ed and other photo-worthy events. I have to admit I was somewhat insulted! I may not have worn as much makeup as models did back then, but I was just me, and I thought I had the makings of a model.

My only other option at the time seemed to be to use my degree to teach, but I still wasn't moved to follow that path quite yet. Stalling about what to do with my life, I found Frank Fox, the exercise guru of the day. Mr. Fox taught me how to sculpt my body down to its optimal physical condition. Even if I couldn't be in front of the camera or on the stage, I wanted to look my best. I worked with him three times a week and walked for an hour every day along the lake. It was hard work, but by the end of three months, I had changed the entire shape of my body, including my disdained chubby legs.

It paid off when I got a call from a man who introduced himself as Norm Cahners of Bangor, Maine. He was in town with his father at a furniture convention and had read about me at the World's Fair in the newspaper. He was so enthusiastic and brash that he asked to have dinner with me. I was intrigued by his confidence but admitted that I didn't know whether I wanted to accept his invitation.

He said, "I guarantee you will be glad you did," and my curiosity got the best of me. I said yes. When he came to pick me up, he revealed himself to be an enthralling young man, oozing charm. He had a taxi waiting downstairs, which seemed very extravagant. At dinner we talked for hours. He had been on the Harvard University track team and qualified for the 1936 Olympics, which he subsequently chose to boycott. He was tall, blond, and twenty-six years old. I was twenty-one and had never met anybody quite that cocky, glib, or slick. I fell for him right away.

When he asked, I agreed to have lunch with him and his father the next day. Mr. Cahners told me that he had three sons, one daughter, and his own furniture business. He asked about me and my family. I didn't realize that the meeting was an interview, but apparently I passed. When the business trip was over and Norm went back to Maine, we kept in touch through letters.

We would be geographically reunited when I accepted an invitation to travel with my Uncle Sam. After all these years, Uncle Sam was still living with us. He was fun, and I enjoyed his company. We took the train to Jacksonville, Florida, rented a car, and drove down the coastal highway. In Ft. Lauderdale, I walked into the Hollywood Hotel, and there was Norm! I had known he would be in Florida at the time, but this meeting was completely serendipitous. I couldn't believe the coincidence or my good luck. What was it with all these wonderful men unexpectedly popping up in my life?

After my time in New York and to celebrate my graduation, my travels continued, this time to Florida, with my Uncle Sam. He was a great companion, and we had a wonderful time traversing the Atlantic Coast together.

Norm took me sailing the next day. It was magnificent—the blue skies, the clear water, the wind in our faces. I felt like I was in heaven and was having a delightful time. Norm was, too, and suggested that we get married. I thought, "How can you talk like that, you cocky bastard?" Still, I was intrigued.

The next day I said a temporary good-bye to Norm, and Uncle Sam and I took off for the rest of our trip. In Daytona Beach, Uncle Sam taught me how to ride a bike, and in Palm Beach, I taught him how to dress. We stayed in Palm Beach at an extravagant manor called the Whitehall, built around a large open-air central courtyard. The whole trip was an amazing time!

Once I returned from Florida, my travels continued when later that summer Mother and I returned to New York, where I connected with Norm once again. As we were wont to do, he and I had nonstop fun and took in the sights. I even visited with Orvil, who was married by then, and wished him well. (As fate would have it, he married the newspaper heiress Marian Sulzberger and became the publisher of *The New York Times*. "If I don't have one Marion, I'll get another," he joked.)

Then Norm and I left Mother in New York and went to Boston to visit his sister. On our side trip, the romance deepened. After dinner with his family one night, Norm and I went on the porch and got hot and heavy. I had never given in to anybody, but I was very close to giving in to him. He was, at turns, persuasive, demanding, sensual, and insistent. I have to say I was not unenthusiastic myself. But the housekeeper walked in on us, and the interruption stopped the whole business. Later, sleeping in my own bed, I was a little shaken by his desires as well as my own.

We returned to New York, and Norm issued another invitation to travel, this time to Bangor, Maine. He wanted me and my mother to come and meet his family. "I want you to marry me," he said. "We'll announce it in September."

As I think about it now, even that was brash. He didn't ask me to marry him—he simply assumed I would. Still, at the time, I was pretty crazy about him and was overtaken by physical yearning and romantic fantasies. He had a powerful effect on me. I had nervous butterflies in my stomach the entire ride to Maine. As it turned out, I had good reason to worry.

Norm's mother was pleasant in a professional and mannered way that let me know she was evaluating Mother and me carefully. Mrs. Cahners had long ago decided that her sons were valuable commodities, and she was determined that all three of them marry wealthy girls. Mergers of this sort were not at all uncommon during this volatile time, but they usually were largely unspoken.

The reception of us, the scrutiny toward us, inside the lovely Cahners home was chilly—hardly the behavior of a family of future in-laws. My mother was ice-cold as well. To begin with, the last thing in the world she wanted was for me to move to Maine. Worse, she bristled at the naked audacity of their interviewing style and was somewhat intimidated. Although my mother could easily have measured up to anyone in terms of intelligence and style, she felt her limited education like an open wound, and when the Cahnerses probed that sore, she dove inward.

Even his grandmother, who had an accent like my own grandmother's, didn't relieve my mother's social anxiety and measuring stick. We were more like them than they thought, but they were nothing like us. The visit was very uncomfortable.

I was stuck in between all of it, with my attention focused mainly on Norm. Although we managed to get away for some necking, the emotional temperature of the weekend was cool. Once back home,

I didn't tell anyone of my soon-to-be-announced engagement. I must have sensed that something was wrong. I also continued to stall on my decision about teaching. I was confused about seemingly everything in my life at this point.

Eventually, I got a "Dear Marion" letter from Norm. His father had apparently paid for a Dun and Bradstreet report on my father's assets, and we had come up insufficient in their estimation. I was mortified and sobbed rivers into the tiled bathroom across from my bedroom in Hyde Park. After two decades of being a lady, smiling when I was forced to give up things I wanted and having my life basically laid out before me, my tears somehow represented my sorrow about more than just the callousness of the Cahners family.

PART III

BUILDING A FAMILY—AND A CAREER

Marriage, Maybe

Following the experience with Norm and his family, I found myself feeling less compliant in terms of other people making decisions for me. After giving up the stage, as well as a serendipitous opportunity in motion pictures, studying where and what my parents wanted, losing Alan Tishman, and being jilted by Norm Cahners, I simply refused to let my work be chosen for me. I turned down a teaching position in southern Illinois and became a full-time professional volunteer for the American Red Cross.

Although the United States hadn't declared war yet, working at the Red Cross made me feel as if I was helping the effort overseas and at home in Chicago. I offered my time and became the administrative assistant to the head volunteer. Society ladies from Lake Forest ran the organization effectively and with panache. They were competent, polite, and pleasant, women who would be running corporations today. Then, however, they were merely management volunteers but were viewed with a manner of respect, as everyone was starting to pull together for the benefit of the country.

As a volunteer I was given courses in office procedures, including typing, filing, and translation. I helped to run the information booth and library services and served at army containments, hospitals, and other agencies as needed. There was never a lack of things to do, and I enjoyed doing everything, even separating yarn and distributing it to make sweaters sent overseas. As a staff assistant, I drove important people from the Red Cross, as well as other military professionals, around town. I took a turn working at seemingly every department on every floor of the building. It was multitasking before there was such a thing, and I felt as if I was doing something to make a difference.

In June of 1942, while I was hard at work at the Red Cross, Bud Simon came home for a few days to take my romantic temperature. After graduating from Brown University, he had joined the air force and was one of the early flyboys trained at Randolph Field in Texas. By the time I saw him, he was stationed at Williams Field in Arizona and training to command fighter planes. It was thrilling to see him dressed in his crisp air force uniform and filled with delight. I was in awe of him and the rest of the guys like him who had joined the war effort early. They were fascinating and fearless, loved what they were doing, and lived for it.

At dinner at the Pump Room at the Ambassador East Hotel, he told me that he had been disappointed that during my trip to California I hadn't surprised him with a visit while he was training in San Francisco. In some romantic delusion, he said he had gone so far as to wait at the rooftop restaurant at the Mark Hopkins Hotel—hoping (like Bogart) that out of all the gin joints in all the towns, I would choose his.

He asked me to marry him again. I don't remember what he said exactly, but I decided that unlike Norm, Bud really meant it. I realized I loved him and probably always had. After all, he was a constant in my life and had stayed loyal to me no matter whom I had been off with at the moment. He was asking for my hand—not demanding it. By then I had had sufficient experiences with men, and I could plainly distinguish between infatuation and love, desire and commitment. Bud definitely embodied the latter, and I trusted him.

Even though I wasn't passionately stirred the way I had been with Alan or Norm, I knew that with Bud our affections and friendship were genuine. I also knew my mother and grandmother would approve. I said yes. The date was June 17, 1942, which happened to be my parents' wedding anniversary. However, despite my engagement, once again, I didn't tell anyone or make any plans. I didn't want to be rash and was still evaluating my true feelings. It had been some time since I had seen Bud, and I didn't necessarily want to rush into anything based purely on emotional pull. I had to be rational.

When Bud Simon next appeared in my life, he had joined the air force. He looked thrillingly handsome in his uniform, and I was so happy to see him. He asked me to marry him, and I said yes.

Bud returned to Arizona. Two months passed, and in his absence I continued to question my decision. For my birthday in August, he sent me a gorgeous ring, which I wore around my neck to avoid questions. When my mother discovered the ring, she said, "You can't accept anything like that until you're ready to marry him." The entire ordeal made me so nervous that I developed a sinus problem. And where do you send somebody for sinus, if not Arizona? We decided to take a trip west to meet with Bud and clear up my illness and my head.

Bud met Mother and me in Phoenix, and when I saw him, I instantly knew he was the man I wanted to marry. After so much time apart, all my doubts disappeared when we were reunited in person. He took us for a ride in his plane. It was thrilling beyond belief. He was excited, I was excited, Mother was excited. Caught up in the moment, by the time we landed, I suggested that December might be a good time to get married. However, Bud's schedule moved it up. He had a ten-day leave coming up and told me that we'd have to get married right away so we would be able to enjoy a honeymoon while he had time off.

It was terribly romantic to get married so quickly after waiting so long, and I felt deeply flattered that he had been pining after me for several years. Somehow in that little window of time during my Southwest visit—just ten days—we planned a wedding and picked out a house to live in, in Phoenix, after our honeymoon.

My mother and I took the train to Los Angeles to shop for my dress at Saks Fifth Avenue. We chose a gorgeous long-sleeved gown with a heart-shaped neckline—price tag, $39. It was the smallest size they had in stock in the store, so we could take it back to Arizona to use immediately without any alterations. I did my own hair and makeup and made most of the arrangements for the day, even taking time to help my mother and father with various last-minute tasks. The time frame was short, but we pulled together an elegant event that I will always remember. On Sunday afternoon, October 25, I married Bud Simon by candlelight amid many gorgeous flower arrangements in Phoenix's Westward Ho Hotel. Our guests—thirty-two in all—were my parents, Uncle Sam, Bud's parents, his Aunt Peggy, his brother Bill, and all of his air force buddies.

Bud Simon and I were married in an intimate candlelit ceremony on October 25, 1942.

On a trip to visit Bud in Arizona with my mother, we planned a spontaneous wedding in the span of a few days. My dress came from Saks Fifth Avenue in Los Angeles.

The Simons were not as calculating in advancing their social status as the Cahnerses had been, but the family was no less significant. Bud's father, William, had been at the helm of the American Metal Company for years. His mother, Celeste Weil Simon, was a member of the Stix family, of Stix, Baer, and Fuller, a St. Louis store similar to Marshall Field's.

Bud was not a very religious man, so for the ceremony, he had asked the rabbi not to use Hebrew—but he slipped up. After the rabbi's first "mitzvah" and "mazel tov," I watched as Bud's neck got redder and redder. I couldn't contain my amusement, and a fit of giggles caused my veil to bounce up and down. My mother was not pleased with my outburst.

Afterward we celebrated with an intimate dinner. My father made a toast with a bottle of champagne from the case he had brought from Chicago. Sugar was being rationed at the time, so our wedding cake was small—but delicious. It was topped with a plastic soldier and a bride. The whole evening was fun, elegant, and memorable. Then, the next morning, when I came down for breakfast, with my parents and my new in-laws staying in the same hotel, I felt as if I was wearing a sign that read: "I'm not a virgin anymore!"

Our wedding was small, with only thirty-two guests. After the ceremony, we celebrated with a lovely dinner for our guests.

Bud and I were happy, as newlyweds usually are. We honeymooned at the Lone Palm in Palm Springs, California, which was chock-full of celebrities to watch. Alan Ladd was impressed with Bud's diving skills. John Garfield was there with one of his kids. Al Jolson took any gathering of people to be an audience and got up and performed.

We spent most of the time in our cottage, and when we did get out to explore, we got teased a lot because we both looked so young. We were only in our midtwenties but must have looked like teenagers. We swam, lounged in the sun, enjoyed each other, and ate at the Brown Derby in L.A. It was lovely. I felt certain that I had made the right choice and was embarking on a wonderful new life.

War Bride, War Mother

Bud and I settled in to our new married life in Arizona. Living away from home and in a strange environment was a new experience for me, as was being the wife of a flyboy. Bud's shift was continually changing so he could master various flying conditions. He usually got up at 4 a.m. and was home around 1 p.m., so we were at least able to spend the day together. Because we didn't have an alarm clock when we first moved in, I asked the hotel where we had our wedding to give us wake-up calls. We were in great shape financially because Bud was earning a living that supported us and he had extra income from his father's stocks as well. We rented a nice house with a fenced-in yard and a garden in a lovely neighborhood. I even had a piano to play, which came with the house.

Bud and I started our married life in this home in Arizona. It was exciting, but at the same time, I felt somewhat lonely because I didn't know anyone and missed my family.

Everything was exciting but also oddly scary and somewhat overwhelming. After a lifetime of being surrounded by people I knew—through school, clubs, social events, various networks—I found myself living in a place where nobody knew me. I didn't have a single person to call, and long distance was expensive. In the mornings, while Bud was gone, I'd visit with my neighbor while she hung out the laundry, just to have somebody to talk to.

I wasn't necessarily lonely. As an only child, I was used to being self-sufficient and finding things to do. In the quiet time I spent at home while Bud was away, I played piano, took a home course in interior decorating and one on writing through *The New York Times*, read, and cooked a lot. But life was different and required adjustment.

While most of the country was rationing everything from gas to sugar, we were thankful that our deprivation was relatively limited. Because Bud was part of the war effort, he got whatever gas he needed to take him back and forth to the base, and even our diet changed very little despite the rationing. If we had enough time between Bud's shifts, we even went out to restaurants for dinner now and then, although there weren't that many places to go in Phoenix at that time (population 63,000).

Even though Bud's schedule was full with all of his flyboy training, we managed to spend our afternoons together.

Because Bud was the first one of his friends to be married, our house became the unofficial officer's club—the place to be. I took on the role of entertainer and welcomed the distraction from my quiet days. Our parties were memorable! Every now and then, one of Bud's flyboy friends would get a supply of steaks reserved for servicemen and we would have a cookout. During the rare periods when the guys were off duty together, they drank themselves stupid and were hung over the next day. But we all had a good time and relished the lighthearted feelings of freedom.

At Christmas, I upped my entertaining ante and invited thirty people over for dinner, which required borrowing the refrigerator of a neighbor. I wanted to do things like my mother did, so I prepared a huge fruit platter, soup, turkey, shrimp, and two desserts and brought in some-body to help me with washing dishes. Everything was prepared in advance so that Bud and I could enjoy Christmas Eve together.

As it turned out, Bud and I had too good a time on December 24. We ate lobster and drank far too much champagne. In the morning I felt terrible. Of course I was hung over, but that idea was so horrific and unthinkable to me that Bud kindly told me that I probably had a touch of the flu and I believed him. If I had thought that I had done something to bring on the sickness, I would have been furious with myself. He brought me tea and toast, and slowly as the day went on, I revived—about a half hour before our guests arrived.

The pleasant winter in the West wore on, and in the spring Bud and I took a trip to Los Angeles. I didn't feel well during the whole trip. At the Brown Derby I was particularly ill and wanted to leave. Bud seemed annoyed because he wanted to sit and ogle Olivia de Havilland, who was at the restaurant. Graciously, one of the guys in our party, an actor named Georgie Stone, offered to come outside with me to get some air. While we were walking, he said, "This always happens with your first one." I was initially shocked at his implication but then became giddy at the prospect of being pregnant. Soon after, it was confirmed that I was expecting my first child. I was delighted, and so was Bud.

I had a very easy pregnancy, other than my initial episode, and felt simply marvelous the entire time. It was 117 degrees day after day, and we didn't have air-conditioning, but I didn't care! I was young and happy. Strangely, I barely even showed until the very end.

In due time, Bud and I found out we were expecting our first child. I hardly showed (this picture is of me at three months), and my pregnancy was very easy—up to the delivery.

The ease of pregnancy ended at the time of delivery. My labor was extremely difficult and lasted for two long days. My darling daughter Kathy was born on December 7, 1943, two years to the day after the attack on Pearl Harbor. Despite the joyous occasion of her arrival, the delivery seemed to foreshadow a series of sneak attacks on my life and well-being, as well as hers.

Kathy's first few days were shaky. Unsanitary conditions at the hospital created an environment that caused her to become covered with little sores called impetigo. She cried. She refused to nurse. She cried more. I was in a state as well. My stitches became inflamed, and my nipples were raw. However, these were minor irritations compared to my mental condition. I suddenly began to feel as though I was hallucinating.

The world looked out of shape to me. Wavy. Watery. I was confused. I looked at people and they seemed out of sync. Faces appeared off-kilter and frightening. I was very disturbed and tried to help myself in any way I could think of. I took hot and cold showers in hopes that I would shock myself back to being normal. Once I returned home, I walked around the backyard while stomping my feet. I did whatever I thought I could or should do to knock myself back into the state of mind I was accustomed to.

Nothing worked. My symptoms escalated, along with my terror. There was a hospital for the emotionally disturbed that we would pass on the highway, during which times I silently declared, "I'm never going near you. I'll take care of this myself." But I knew something was out of whack. I was extremely anxious all the time.

Bud was very supportive while I endured this difficult time, and he developed a special bond with Kathy while I was unable to mother her as I would have if I hadn't been so confused and scared.

Occasionally, the symptoms would lift. I'd feel fine and hope the ordeal was over. I'd visit with other young mothers and drink sherry in the afternoons. Everything seemed as if it was going to be OK. I had a lovely baby. I had a community of mothers. And by the time our husbands got home, thanks to the sherry, we were carefree and loved them dearly.

Cruelly, the symptoms came back. I was at my wit's end. Uncle Sam came to visit, and I poured out my heart, and my list of symptoms, to him. He reassured me that what I had was a condition called postpartum depression. He had heard about it from a friend who was the head of psychiatry at the University of Illinois. It was supposed to be something you just got over—but I didn't.

Then, to make matters worse, physical pain began to assault my body. I experienced what felt like a band of steel around my abdomen.

It got so bad that I would keel over in agony, afraid I was going to faint. Between the world looking odd and my body feeling awful, I got even more upset and anxious. I got dizzy and panicky. I was afraid to be alone with the baby.

That's when Bud and I decided that it was time to go home, back to Chicago. The family could meet Kathy and I some doctors. As soon as we got to my parents' apartment, which Uncle Sam had finally vacated after I got married, I went to Michael Reese Hospital for an evaluation. I'll never forget going for x-rays in the basement of the hospital. There I was, a young healthy-looking girl on the outside in the midst of a lot of older sick people.

Because MRIs did not exist in those days, doctors couldn't find anything wrong with me. On the basis of the severity of the symptoms and absence of imaging information, they decided to perform an exploratory operation. During the procedure, it was discovered that I had an adhesion from my stomach to my gallbladder that had been caused by the pregnancy. As my physicians explained it, when I was anxious, I would swallow air, which pulled the adhesion. So the offending culprit was removed, as well as my appendix for good luck.

The surgery relieved my physical pain; however, it was no cure for my psychological problems. I continued to feel anxious and feared something was really wrong with me mentally. I knew I could not go back to Phoenix until I felt better. I didn't want to live in a fog, and I knew that I couldn't take care of a child without being able to think properly. So I talked to my internist, who, thankfully, had been through psychoanalysis. He suggested that I do the same. I agreed to follow his orders and asked for a referral.

Finding Myself

The next day Bud and I found ourselves face-to-face with the legendary creative pioneer of psychoanalysis herself, Therese Benedek. Like my dance and piano teachers, Therese was from Europe. While still at the Gymnasium in Budapest, she became so inspired by the new ideas coming out of Vienna about dreams that she decided to become a doctor.

After undergoing psychoanalysis with the famous Sándor Ferenczi, Therese began analysis on patients at the then newly established Berlin Institute. In 1933, she emigrated with her husband and their two children to the United States. At the Chicago Institute of Psychoanalysis she participated in research on psychosomatic medicine and eventually became famous for her formidable intuition, idiosyncratic style, and independent mind.

Therese Benedek would come to develop an intuitive, magical capacity to know how her patients felt even when they could not articulate their feelings. By the time I met her, she was nearly fifty years old and well on her way to becoming the legend in her field that she is today. Yet, initially Bud and I fooled her. Because I was composed and smiling when we met, she assumed that Bud was the patient.

I trusted Therese immediately. Fashionable and austere, she gave the impression of no-nonsense competence in a very tiny and quiet persona. After a few minutes of conversation, I decided to go for it. I felt that I didn't have anything to lose and wanted to get it over with fast so I could get back to Bud and Kathy and our life in Phoenix. Little did I know how quickly I would acclimate to the therapy or how much it would help me in the end.

For the next three months, I went to talk to Therese every day. I didn't tell anyone what I was doing. Seeing a psychiatrist was neither understood nor socially acceptable at that time. During the week, I went to Therese's office downtown in anonymity. On weekends, to keep from being seen entering the famous psychiatrist's home around the corner from my mother's apartment, I would quietly slip in the back door.

Although my mother had probably been through severe postpartum depression herself, when she found out what I was doing, she was shocked beyond words that her perfect child had anything wrong with her. She was less than thrilled with my decision to see Therese, but, perhaps for the first time, I didn't care how my mother felt about my choices. I was a mother myself, and I was too sick to focus on my child. The opportunity to work on myself so I could raise and nurture that child held great promise.

At that point, I didn't really care about what other people thought; I just wanted to know what I thought! More than anything, I wanted to stop feeling as if I was hallucinating. I also began to want to understand myself. Like a faucet, ready and willing, I poured out things about my life that I had not previously examined.

We began slowly. I would look at the painting above Therese's couch and tell her whatever came into my mind. We talked about what those ideas, feelings, fantasies, and memories meant. Before long we were talking about my mother's withdrawn personality. Her strictness. My compliance. My father's benign distance. We talked about the couple mother and I stayed with in California when I was five years old. The difference between this very seductive Frenchman and my father. How I felt about his attention.

We talked about how I felt about submission. Love. Control. Respect. Duty. Conformity. Loss. Disappointment. Expectations.

We talked about the terror and triumphs of performing on the stage and my feelings of sudden loss in having it taken away from me. We talked about how dieting changed the way men related to me. We talked about obedience and the consequences of it, my fear of conflict.

About not pursuing a career in the movies. About how I'd even studied what my mother selected. My feelings about my boyfriends and men in general. I had had an abundance of male attention, yet I couldn't capture the man I thought I wanted: Alan Tishman. We talked about Norm and about thrilling sensations, loss, and shame. We talked about Bud and loyalty. Friendship. I loved Bud and always had, but it wasn't the kind of romantic excitement that I wanted to feel. I considered how Bud and I were such good friends for so many years that it seemed natural to comply with his wishes and desires, in order to make him happy.

Therapy with Therese was like a master's course in understanding myself. I would leave her office, go home, dream, and come back, and we would discuss it. I was remembering things that I had no idea had upset me, things that I had no idea had affected my life in the present moment.

As I did the tough mental work, at first, my anxiety level seemed to worsen. I would go into a department store and get panicky for no apparent reason. I had intense panic attacks on a couple of occasions while I was with my mother. I understood that it was other people's attempt to control me that had such a profound effect. Once, I had to be a perfect child; I now had to be a perfect adult. I had made my mother's expectations my own. I don't think I even knew how to distinguish between my own feelings and hers.

At the end of my three months with Therese, I was finally feeling good enough to go back to Arizona. The therapy had worked. I was proud to have beaten my illness and discovered myself in the process, but I was saddened to leave Therese, though we continued to work together by mail.

Moving Matters

Back at our home in the desert, I finally started to realize how lucky I was, how lucky Bud and I were. We had a beautiful place to live and a burgeoning new family. I loved my little girl with all my heart. Kathy was such a wonderful baby that it was as though a golden light surrounded her. At ten months she took her first steps and began running right after that. She never stopped. She was so tiny and talked at such a young age that it was hard to believe that those words, and corresponding ideas, were coming out of that little child.

Because we spent so much time in our garden, one of the first words she ever said was "flower." When she was about sixteen months old, she brought me a bouquet of flowers that she had assembled herself. Her sense of color and aesthetic appreciation and even her concentration were amazing.

Kathy was a marvelous child and reached milestones quickly. Her first word was "flower" at eleven months.

As life went on, I was feeling so good, and Kathy was such a pleasure, that I decided to try to get pregnant again. Because of my recent surgery, it was not recommended, but Bud and I both wanted more than one child and decided to risk it. In the spring of 1945, we were thrilled to discover that I was expecting again. This time, however, it was Bud who ended up in the hospital.

During a routine pressure test, a tiny blister ruptured and Bud's lung collapsed. He was rushed to the hospital in Phoenix, where they discovered that he had tuberculosis. By the time I got to the hospital, Bud was already aware of his diagnosis. He was in anguish, both physically and mentally. He knew that the career and the life he loved were over. An extreme depression overtook him. As the weeks went by, with each visit, Kathy and I watched as his appearance diminished. Along with his shrinking sense of self, he lost interest in our lives and in us.

During Bud's time in the hospital, Kathy was only eighteen months old, and she became easily upset because her daddy wasn't able to pick her up or show her much attention. While I was sick after her birth, Bud had been doubly attentive. The two were very close and shared a special bond. He had always bounced her in his lap and played with her. She didn't understand why she couldn't be with him. In his mentally and physically weakened state, he barely noticed her. He wasn't paying much attention to me, either.

Bud asked me to take Kathy and return to Chicago, where he wanted his family to take care of us. I wanted to stay in Phoenix, but he insisted that Kathy and I leave. I think he felt that if we were with his parents, then on some level he would still be taking care of us. I also think he didn't want us to see him the way he was. He clearly didn't have the energy to pretend he felt anything but devastated. I felt so sorry for him that I went along with what he wanted.

In June of 1945, Kathy, our housekeeper, and I moved our entire household, including a dog we had adopted from a friend, into my mother-in-law, Celeste's, big colonial house in suburban Glencoe. Twelve richly ornamented rooms with elaborate chandeliers, beautiful cornices, and great marble fireplaces became our residence. It was a stark difference from our simple Southwestern-style house. We were thankful for his family's graciousness and the opulent surroundings, but we did not enjoy living there at the time.

Celeste questioned many of my parenting decisions and ran the house like an army general. My days were spent trying to stay out of her way, and my nights were spent over long and large meals that she planned and we ate in polite but frosty cordiality. I often retreated from the stress to visit and play with Kathy. Socializing didn't appeal to me much at the time. I yearned to get back to my own life, back to normalcy.

On Thursdays, Mother took the train to visit us, but her presence in the big house served only to complicate the situation further. There was quiet but tense competition between my mother and Celeste. Celeste had more money and social status; my mother was a snob and felt inferior. It was a shame. Mother was bright, and she had a nice husband who had a successful business. She didn't have to work and had household help. She could have gone back to school at any time but instead sunk into depression and silence. Needless to say, the tension in the house when the two women were there was almost unbearable.

To complicate things more, Bud was being moved around at that time. First, he was transferred to a hospital in Tucson and later to Fitzsimons Hospital in Denver, which was the top army hospital for patients with tuberculosis. Once I took Kathy and visited Bud in Denver. The minute I saw him it was obvious that his depression had progressed as my pregnancy had: quietly, steadily, and, finally, observably. He had begun to sneak Scotch into his afternoon milk to dull his pain. My pain, however, was undiluted.

As soon as I got out of his room and away from Kathy, I sobbed and sobbed. I felt so much sorrow for Bud. I knew how much he had loved flying, and I knew it was over. Worse, I could not deny that some essential part of Bud was over as well. On the plane ride home, I dried my tears and decided to focus on finding us a home of our own. I may have had to live with a depressed husband, but I didn't have to do it in the same house as a domineering mother-in-law.

A New Dawn and Direction

On January 29, 1946, Bud retired from the air force, was released from Fitzsimons Hospital, and was put on a plane to Chicago. From the moment he arrived, I could see that he didn't give a hoot about seeing us. He was very weak and needed another six months of bed rest, but the problem was far greater than fatigue. He had totally withdrawn. I was nine months pregnant and looking at a husband who was a stranger to me. There was no evidence of the man who had once been full of life and adventure. The man who was my enthusiastic friend, my joyous flyboy husband, was gone. I think the shock brought on my labor.

Our daughter Toni was born two days later, in the middle of a blizzard. Just as during Kathy's birth, I was alone. Bud was not allowed to get out of bed to observe the miraculous moment. Although I was thrilled to have another daughter, I was more focused on Bud's lack of attention than I was on our new baby. Though I knew it to be true, it somehow hadn't yet sunk in that Bud was never again going to be the man I married.

Our second daughter, Toni, was born in the middle of a blizzard in January 1946.

I was fortunate enough to be able to bring a nurse home from the hospital to help me, which was the old-fashioned way. It was that nurse who told me without mincing words: "Look, either you want to get upset or you want to feed your kid. Be upset later and feed your kid now." I saw her reasoning and acted accordingly. After all, no matter how distant Bud was, or how ill, we had two children, and we both owed them a happy life.

To get on with my own life I formed a team of allies. First, I started to build myself back up by starting with my body. After losing the attention of my husband and gaining weight through all the months of Celeste's formal dinners, I called upon my old friend Frank Fox to help readjust my figure.

"What did you do to yourself?" he bluntly asked me when he saw my postbaby/four-course-meals figure. Then he gave me specific exercises to do three times a week. Fox was strict but effective, and I, as always, was a disciplined student. In six weeks the results were unbelievable. I looked better than I had before I was pregnant.

Another member of the team came from a source closer to home. Bud's brother, Corporal Billy Simon, had returned from Belgium, thus making the house even more crowded; the two of us, however, became good friends. We had no one other than each other to turn to. Bud was Celeste's favorite child, and their sister Libby was their father's favorite.

Rounding out my support group were a Realtor and a decorator. The Realtor was like a constant companion. Kathy looked at so many houses with us that for years she thought that if you went to someone's house, you had to go up to the top and down to the basement to see everything. Her exposure to real estate and decisions about décor may have contributed to her success as an interior designer later in life.

I had to fight Celeste to keep my decorator. She wanted me to use her decorator and was extremely critical of all the things I brought home to show Bud. For his part, Bud was remote and equally critical of my efforts and tended to side with his mother. Fortunately, I was long past someone else making my decisions for me and found the courage to stick with my own taste. Still, it was a very lonely, contentious time in my life.

Eventually, I found a house in Winnetka that I loved: a three-story colonial situated on a large yard with lots of trees and surrounded by a white picket fence. It was postcard Americana. I wasn't asking anybody for permission, least of all my mother-in-law. After being a "good girl" and acquiescing far too many times in my life, I was not going to let my dream house turn into a nightmare. I made the decision without Bud's input. My father-in-law gently asked me whether I was certain I wanted to spend that much. I admitted that I wasn't sure but told him that it had two fireplaces and window seats and was walking distance to the train, the grammar school, and the little village center. Whatever his reservations, Bud's father kept the promise he had made to me so many summers ago when I first met Bud, and he bought us the house.

We moved in August of 1946, two months after Bud finally got out of bed. A modern kitchen, large living and dining rooms, and a porch that I would eventually enclose to make an extra room were located on the first floor. On the second floor there was a master bedroom, dressing room, bathroom, and den, along with a bedroom for each of the girls and a bath in between. The third floor became a playroom. There was also a basement with a laundry room and enough space to one day accommodate the two additional children we hoped for. On my decorator's advice, I selected beautiful furnishings for the first floor. To this day I still have all the lovely furniture I bought more than sixty-five years ago for my first real home.

Cracks in the Castle

From the outside, our family must have looked like an advertisement for the American dream: two attractive parents, two beautiful children, a tasteful home with a white picket fence, and a maid to make sure that everyone and everything continued to look beautiful. The reality was, as it sometimes is, quite different.

After his long convalescence, Bud finally went to work for my uncles at their photographic supply company. I was grateful to them for making a place for him. It was a fantastic opportunity because my uncles had no kids to leave their company to and it was a very big business.

Unfortunately, it wasn't a good fit. Bud wasn't a photographer or a merchant. In his heart, he was an adventurer, a hunter, an explorer—a flyer. And working nine to five in a job—any job—diminished what was left of him even further. Instead of brimming with enthusiasm for the opportunity that had been handed to him, Bud was seething with a low-level anger at his physical limitations, missing the excitement and drama of the air force and bored and resentful of the tedium of working a "regular" job. Bristling at the idea of taking orders, he refused to accommodate the desires of his in-law employers. Instead, he quietly began a habit of martini lunches that did not sit well with my uncles.

In December, at eleven months old, Toni started eating real food and got immediately and violently sick. She had mucus in her stool and tremendous cramps, and she cried constantly. The doctors at Children's Memorial Hospital were baffled. Although they had seen other babies suffering from the same symptoms—and even knew that some were dying because they couldn't absorb their food—they didn't know what caused the problem.

Eventually—much later—they determined that Toni was suffering from celiac disease, an intolerance to gluten that causes the body to respond to its presence by damaging the small intestine and preventing the absorption of essential nutrients. Without knowing the cause of her condition at the time or being able to give a definitive diagnosis, Toni's doctors implemented a successful treatment of eliminating gluten—along with almost everything else—in her diet. We put her on a daily regimen of six bananas and milk with mild doses of phenobarbital to calm her down. She ate that—and only that—for a year. Her overall diet was limited for five long years, and while tending to her strict nutritional needs was difficult, we saw that the change eventually did seem to help.

As Toni got better physically, she began to develop a powerful will as well as a temper that wouldn't fully reveal itself until she was an adult. Not to be outdone, Kathy got pneumonia and was understandably cranky. To keep her from being hospitalized, which I thought would be too psychologically traumatic, I had to learn how to inject her every three hours with penicillin by practicing on an orange.

Despite some trying physical difficulties in their early years, Kathy and Toni formed a strong bond. They played house and often ate dinner upstairs together.

The first few years in our own home were trying. We had problems—but all people have problems, don't they? As a young couple just getting over Bud's illness, we struggled to deal with our children's medical issues as well. During that time I made the best of a difficult situation by volunteering at the Winnetka Children's Fair and the Hubbard Woods PTA. I was energized by the work, but Bud and the girls wore me out. Yet, looking at photographs of our family at the time, it's impossible to tell that we had any problems at all. Cherubic little girls, in matching dresses, flank their well-dressed parents like beautiful dolls. The physical, and sometimes emotional, problems that plagued each of us are well hidden beneath a façade of elegant living. But the house with the white picket fence, the money, and the help couldn't shield any of us from the reality of difficulties and disappointments.

Our family looked picture perfect—two gorgeous girls and their well-groomed parents. We were happy, but we had our difficulties, as most families do.

Eventually, I, too, came down with something and couldn't get rid of it. I think everything had finally caught up with me, and I was simply exhausted. Bud and my mother sent me to Florida to stay with my mother's best friend. But Aunt Sarah, as I called her, couldn't be bothered with me because she was busy tending to houseguests. She shifted me to the house of her seamstress, an extremely cold Russian woman who was gone all day long. I did nothing but sit alone and cry.

I was such a wreck that my uncles gave Bud time off so that he could join me in Florida. I don't think I was ever so glad to see him, and for the first time in years, he seemed pretty happy as well—for a few days. We went to a hotel in West Palm Beach. I got and stayed drunk as a skunk for four days. We did nothing but drink and make love. It was a temporary cure for what ailed me.

When we returned home, I went back to Therese Benedek, my trusted ally, to try to get my life back on track. She suggested that since

I had done so well in traditional talk therapy, I might try psychoanalysis for a more permanent cure. With Kathy in nursery school, my Uncle Sam provided us with a nurse for Toni so that I could pursue the treatment. Although Toni's cramps were long gone, I was up with her every night for five years because she quickly learned that if she cried, I would come. I was happy to have the time to work on myself and hopefully make my family happy and whole again.

Going Deeper

Psychoanalysis turned out to be far more intensive, intrusive, and interesting than talk therapy had been. I engaged in the exploratory process for a year and a half, and it was worth every second.

Based on our previous experience together, I greatly admired and trusted Therese. In the process of therapy I told her my dreams and fantasies. I talked about everything and anything that came into my head as she patiently formulated the unconscious conflicts that caused my symptoms and problems. I didn't fool around; I wanted to learn from psychoanalysis, and I was a dutiful "patient," but I didn't want to depend on it.

Because psychoanalysis seeks to clarify connections among unconscious components of mental processes, my meetings with Therese, our conversations, felt like a secret voyage into the world of me that I had no idea existed. It went so much deeper than the talk therapy. Our new goal was to reveal unconscious symbolic reactions stimulated by my experiences. I verbalized not just the facts of my life as I remembered them but also my thoughts and feelings about those facts.

Although we had already talked about my mother's depression, my discipline, my father's limited presence, my compliance as a girl, and my loves and losses, this time we started to speculate on how I felt and the reasons I might have responded the way I did to all of these situations on an unconscious level. Why was I so uncomfortable with Slim's French husband? How might that have affected my self-image? How might that have affected my feelings about being a character performing on a stage? And giving it up?

I'll never forget the feeling of having had my insides scraped out. After some particularly deep sessions, I'd walk around wondering whether I would be able to fill myself up again. Toward the end, I felt light. Empty. Vacant.

But Therese interpreted my life for me in such a way that I had new insights into my problems and myself. We confronted and clarified my well-honed defenses, my resistance to what made me uncomfortable. We looked at the role that guilt played in my life as the overachieving "good girl." Knowledge began to fill the empty spaces. By the time Therese said we didn't have anything else to work on, I felt transparent to myself yet definitely more solid.

Changes

With this newfound self-awareness, I decided that I needed a real change. I enrolled part time in a master's program at my alma mater, the University of Chicago, to pursue my long-relinquished interest in social work. I drove into the city with Bud, dropped him off downtown, and made it to Hyde Park in time for an 8 a.m. class. Afterward, I'd have lunch with my Grandma Bessie, just like old times, and then spend the afternoon at the library.

In one of my social work classes, I learned that patients with TB typically withdraw after being alone in a hospital for extended periods of time. This changed my perspective on Bud's experience, and I became even more sympathetic to what he must have endured. I had just gotten to know myself when I began to understand Bud's drastic change in a new way. But there was no time to focus on either of us, as Kathy suddenly began to change in a severe and disturbing way.

She had gone to Cedar Lake, Wisconsin, with Bud's parents and came back a different child. The change in her demeanor was obvious. Something unspoken had occurred that altered her forever. She never told me what it was, but the effect on her was extreme. It was as if a shade had been drawn; I couldn't reach her no matter what I did. It was unsettling to say the least.

I was extremely worried about my sunshine girl. Because of the analysis I had undergone, I couldn't ignore the repetitive pattern that was forming: first, a withdrawn mother; then, a withdrawn father; and, following, a withdrawn daughter. More significantly, I had been Kathy's exact age—five years old—when I became so uncomfortable and self-conscious staying in California with my mother's friends.

I took Kathy to a child psychiatrist, based on my success with Therese. After an evaluation process that Kathy fought, I was told that she had serious problems. We saw someone else for a second opinion. There, Kathy was offered a dollhouse. She put the parents in the bedroom and the sister in the basement. The doctor said that was typical but told us there was nothing to be done with her at five years old and suggested we bring her back when she was thirteen. This advice was sound at the time, and I trusted the opinion of the doctor, who was highly respected. Also, on the basis of my own previous experience with therapy, I agreed with the decision; a five-year-old would not have the vocabulary or mental capacity to discuss such difficult issues. Instead, I tried my best to return to our usual routine, to make our life as normal as possible for Kathy and the entire family.

I completed my first year of graduate school and expected to work in the field, doing hands-on social work. Instead, the university informed me that there weren't enough supervisors for part-time students, so fieldwork was out of the question. I was disappointed that my alma mater would not support me, but I ended up doing social work anyway: I went to work at Cabrini-Green, the notorious public-housing project in downtown Chicago.

Cabrini-Green

After sidelining my social work education, I expressed my frustration to a friend, Caroline Wallerstein. I told her I wanted to do something where I was actually *doing* it. She said, "I've got just the place for you." Before I knew it, with her help, I was appointed to the Lower North Community Center Board for Cabrini-Green. Still under construction at the time, the public-housing project would, despite great promise, become one of the most infamous, dangerous, and high-profile institutions in America—one that many would identify with violence, poverty, and despair.

By the time I crossed Sedgwick Street for the first time and headed toward the hulking complex, the few whites who initially lived in Cabrini had already fled. As a well-dressed suburban lady, I must have been very conspicuous—but I was never scared, only determined. No classes in social work could have prepared me for what I saw and experienced. Cabrini-Green was like another country—another world—with different customs and a language foreign to me, but I had a job to do, and that's what drove me.

I was so driven that I eventually became president of the board. The annual budget was only $98,000. I wasn't sure what we could do with so little money, but Elliott Donnelley, who chaired other larger-scale community center boards, had passion, personal wealth, and a plan. He got Sidney Epstein and Jay Fox, philanthropists who also supported community centers, to join with us to create the Chicago Youth Centers. By combining talent and finances, we were able to move forward on more solid footing.

Donnelley used his fortune from the R. R. Donnelley printing business to relieve our cash flow crises. Once he gave us $35,000 during a board meeting, which was an enormous amount of money at the time. I got busy spending it, but deciding what to spend it on wasn't easy. There was so much need that it was difficult to know where to begin.

Many of the young women in Cabrini were receiving Aid to Dependent Children. Some had two or three babies in diapers and no reliable source of income. The men who fathered these children were long gone. Appalled but undaunted, I tried to do what seemed most practical in terms of teaching these women how to function outside of their apartments. The idea of taking care of those most at need, most at risk, and most at a loss was something I nurtured. Despite my comfortable upbringing, I knew what it was like to have dreams evaporate. My first challenge at Cabrini was teaching those young women to have dreams. I found that my background in education came in handy, and I put it to use both practically and personally.

To combat their very limited experiences, I worked with a woman named Devorah Sherman to create a small library, leaving a lasting legacy of empowerment through knowledge and learning. Through books, I figured, we could give the young women a chance to imagine a different life and expose them to the idea of choice. Then, once we got them to imagine a life outside of their apartments, we had to teach them how to navigate in the world beyond their front doors. We taught them basic life skills, such as personal hygiene and simple social interaction, including how to place an order in a restaurant.

Controversial in those days was sex education. We added an outpost of Planned Parenthood and brought in a nurse to talk about contraceptives. One girl told me that her parents said she would never make it through school, meaning she would get pregnant and have to drop out. "You can do it," I told her. "It's your choice." She did make it—but first I helped her to imagine her future, and then she decided to live it. Her determination and success propelled me to continue. I was making a difference.

During that time, people living in the projects were noted for telling you they would be somewhere, but then they wouldn't show up. I insisted to all of our students that this was unacceptable. One day a cute little girl came to class and said to me, "Mrs. Simon, I'm sorry I can't be here today." I said, "But you are here." And she said, "You told us to let you know." Then it dawned on me. She didn't have a phone, so she couldn't call, but she made the effort to come and tell me. It was another huge victory that inspired me to do more.

I arranged for someone from Carson Pirie Scott department store to come in and teach the young ladies how to dress in order to get a job. I got Sydney Gordon, a former Powers model, to organize a fashion show. Then I asked all of my friends to donate gently used clothing to sell to the girls. Although we easily could have given the clothes to them, we wanted them to be aware of value for value's sake, so we sold the beautiful dresses for one dollar or fifty cents. We knew that when they used their own money, they would feel ownership and take care of and care about their belongings. At the fashion show itself, they were so excited to be modeling their new clothes. They all looked beautiful. The great sadness was that only two mothers came to see their daughters in the show. The kids were not nearly as disappointed as I was. They didn't expect a lot from their parents, but it still broke my heart.

My hands-on time eventually came to an end when I trained some dedicated and capable women from Cabrini to carry on our instruction and make it their own. Things continued to get worse at the housing project, including gang violence and drugs. All in all I'm proud that I managed to teach a few young women to imagine different lives—in hopes that they could teach their children to imagine different lives and a brighter future. My next steps were in the direction of fund-raising to benefit Cabrini and the Chicago Youth Centers, as well as other social service organizations later on.

Bud's Own Path

As my career was taking off and changing directions, Bud's continued to develop as well. He had quit working for my uncles but had seemingly enjoyed the camera business. He bought his own camera store and ran it himself; he was not really cut out to be an employee working under anyone. I suppose he figured he had the pedigree to manage his own business, with his Brown education, air force experience, and inherent creativity. Maybe he did.

The store, Powell's Camera Mart, on LaSalle off Randolph Street, was in a great location downtown. It had enormous potential, and Bud, as an entrepreneur and his own boss, was initially very passionate. In 1952 he started to get involved with Polaroid and began promoting their instant cameras on television, which at the time was a relatively new phenomenon. To model his cameras in the advertisements, he chose a young woman who worked for him in the store. He had been talking about her for months at dinner at home, proudly telling us that she was bringing in male customers because she was so attractive.

Bud's camera store, Powell's, was a popular destination for photo buffs—including my old dancing teacher, Muriel Abbott (far left)!

At first, I didn't think much about it, but then one day he told me that he had given her a ride home because she had menstrual cramps. I thought to myself, "I don't like it." Talking about her was one thing, but taking her home was another. So I got dressed up and went downtown looking like the boss's wife in a fur wrap and my best jewelry. After discretely assessing her, I decided that I needed to keep my eye on her. I told Bud that if he was so busy with all the new traffic that she was bringing in, I would come in and work in the shop—not that I necessarily wanted to start a new career in photography! I was on a mission to keep my husband. Bud agreed because, as I suspected, he didn't understand what was going on. But I had a pretty good hunch what she was up to.

Sometime after I started to work in the store, another employee told me that he was glad I was there but that the girl was, predictably, very angry about it. Until I got there, she had been the queen bee, and her status had been diminished by my presence. I watched her for a while and confirmed my suspicions: she was sweet on my husband.

I eventually suggested to Bud that I be the one to do the television commercials instead of her. He agreed, so for the next few months, I'd go to Mal Ballairs's studio and demonstrate in front of the television cameras how easy it was to develop the Polaroid pictures.

In the meantime, as I expected, the young girl became discouraged and quit. I had won! I just smiled because Bud still had no idea what was going on.

Bud's downtown store did so well that he opened a second location in Highland Park. He thought of himself as a huge entrepreneur, not just a guy earning a living. Unfortunately, the man he hired to run the LaSalle store was less than trustworthy, and after a few years, Bud had to get rid of both shops—which left him, once again, unemployed.

However, he wasn't worried about money. He was confident that his talent and good luck would carry him onto the next big thing. Instead of pounding the pavement to look for work, he convinced me that he should think about his prospects while skiing in Sun Valley, Idaho, an exciting, brand-new vacation destination at the time. I felt sorry for him and his bad luck, so I was happy to agree to a little getaway if it meant that much to him.

Although Bud had been an avid skier (he even made his own skis while a student at Brown), I was terrified. At the beginning of the trip, he told me to meet him at the restaurant at the top of Bald Mountain. I blithely got on the lift, and as it began to elevate, I became so alarmed I thought I'd have a panic attack. By the time I got to the top, I wanted nothing more than to go back down.

After that, I let Bud teach me to ski, but the combination of horror, dread, and panic each time I had to ascend the mountain on a lift never left me. He enjoyed the challenging slopes while I took beginners' lessons. To distract myself, I would sing or pray out loud while clenching the ski poles and attempting to stay upright. To this day I cannot remember anything that has induced the levels of consistent panic and fear I experienced on the ski lift. But through it all, Bud skied and made friends while I filled the air with terrorized vocal renditions of popular music of the time.

On a trip to Sun Valley, Idaho, I may have been frightened of the ski lifts, but I was not scared of ice-skating! I thought I would be naturally inclined to skate, because of my dancing abilities, but I was wrong! It was much more difficult than I imagined.

The Sun Valley Lodge was famous for meet and greets among the guests. Between dips in the pool, dinners before a roaring fire, and dancing to live music, Bud became acquainted with Eric Lenell of the Maurice Lenell Cookie Company. He made Lenell think that he didn't need to work, which further enticed Lenell's interest in him as a business associate. As it turned out, Bud's creativity and personality were good matches for what Lenell needed, and he offered Bud a job redesigning their packaging to make it more consumer-friendly. In the process, Bud also managed to get the cookies into all of the major grocery store chains. He had fun working for Lenell—for a while.

Although Bud was never out of control with his drinking, he exhibited what we now know to be alcoholic personality traits. Specifically, he bored easily and drank to keep himself in a comfortable haze. Because he was good to me and the girls and never seemed to be out of control, I did my best to ignore the situation for as long as I could.

My Girls

Instead, I focused my attention on my girls and tried to give them the experiences and the freedom that I didn't have while I was growing up. Though my parents were good to me, I never went to camp, but I made sure both of my girls did. I had grown up in an apartment, and I was thrilled to give them a house with a picket fence. Because I never went anywhere without my mother until I got married, I gave them a measure of autonomy that I never had. I also gave them some of the good things that I did have, such as dancing lessons.

Raising my daughters was a source of constant fulfillment. I enjoyed giving them a full and rich childhood, including a trip to summer camp in Maine.

After years at the prestigious Mrs. Wilson's Dancing School, where Bud and I were frequent chaperones, both girls had plenty of dates for parties and dances and proms. The store Young in Heart in Winnetka dressed them like models, and our home was always filled with their friends.

Though they lived much of their lives growing up in parallel, the girls were sometimes stark opposites. They were treated equally, but their reactions to almost everything were as different as day and night—as different as Bud and I were.

Kathy, with her waist-length, wavy reddish-blond hair, was a golden rebel without a cause. She was the child who took off running and never looked back. There were always elements of insecurity and willfulness in her antics. Commanding as much attention as possible, whenever possible, she was never satisfied. Maybe it was because she lost her father's attention at such a young age that she needed everybody else's attention. Maybe it was that unidentified incident at Cedar Lake when she was five. Maybe it was just that she was so much like her father: restless and irresponsible but charming and very bright.

Maybe Kathy also had the predisposition toward the classic alcoholic personality, creating chaos to divert her attention from the fact that she lacked inner peace. Kathy saw herself as the child of an alcoholic. Even though Bud had recovered from TB, he never restored his relationship with his daughter. Kathy seemed to be angry about it, and they fought constantly.

When Kathy turned thirteen years old, I made a conscious decision not to take her back for psychological treatment, but I kept a close watch on her behavior. I was concerned about potential drug use and made her watch a film about a recovering heroin addict with me. While marijuana wasn't yet in vogue, heroin was the drug of choice among the wealthy kids on the North Shore at the time, and I wanted her to see the real effects of the drug. My friends thought it scandalous that I would make a young girl watch that, but I knew I had an addictive child. I don't know how I knew—but I knew. She was like Bud. It turns out I was successful in my mission: she never touched the stuff.

Toni, on the other hand, was a quiet and generally sunny child. Even with her long bout of celiac disease as a baby, she was an easygoing child and very attached to Bud and me. She wouldn't leave my side as a little girl and even held my hand when we went shopping. Despite the fact that she never knew her father before he got sick and never really had his full attention, she worshipped him. And Bud, for his part, glad to have a daughter who didn't challenge him, rewarded her with special activities such as sailing.

But Toni's good cheer continued to be undermined by her physiology. When she was six years old, a strep infection caused her body to hemorrhage into her joints, leaving a trail of blood spackling underneath her skin and causing her to miss a good portion of first grade.

Like Kathy, Toni had started her academic life at Hubbard Woods School in Winnetka. She was consistently an honor student, a wonderful dancer, athletic, popular, and social. Toni loved New Trier High School and was a sweet-faced All-American cheerleader with many, many friends. Unlike Kathy, Toni loved everything about her childhood and hoped to replicate it as an adult someday with a family of her own protected by a white picket fence. She dreamed of growing up to be, well, me.

I was born in Chicago in 1918 and spent most of my childhood and early adulthood on the South Side in Hyde Park.

As a young girl, I developed a strong bond with my father. He was a kind and sensitive man and easily expressed his fatherly instincts.

My mother was an intelligent and stylish woman, yet she was often emotionally distant. However, she supported me in all my endeavors as a child, and we developed a bond over my many activities, such as lessons in dancing and piano.

Working as a full-time professional volunteer for the Red Cross, I honed my multitasking skills. Everything I did helped me feel like I was making a difference.

I took my first trip to Europe in 1959 for five weeks. Traveling then looked different from how it does now—you dressed to impress and wore your finest clothes!

I loved raising my girls, Kathy and Toni. Here we show off our matching mother-daughter outfits from Marion Michaels at my Uncle George Drucker's hundred-acre farm in Deerfield.

Our family represented the typical American dream: a mother, a father, two daughters, and two dogs. The daily reality was sometimes different, but we were still a close-knit unit.

On a trip to California and Arizona when Kathy and Toni were teenagers, we all spent quite a bit of time sunbathing, as was popular at the time. When we returned home, I developed large brown patches on my cheeks and forehead. None of the dermatologists I visited seemed to know what to do. Finally, I went to see a famous chemosurgeon, Dr. Mohs, in Wisconsin. I figured he knew skin better than anyone and would be able to deliver a diagnosis. He did; it was chloasma, which frequently appears in pregnant women (though I was not pregnant!). However, he did not know how to treat it but discussed my case with a colleague, Dr. McCullough, a specialist in pigmentation, who suggested the use of hydroquinone cream. The spots went away after a year of treatment. Needless to say, I no longer spend time in the sun and am a strong advocate of sunscreen.

One of my most highly prized possessions is an antique music stand I acquired with the help of a friend who was an interior designer. It's been a focal point in many of my homes, and I'm always intrigued by its uniqueness. I've never seen anything like it before or since.

To celebrate my fiftieth birthday, our family went on safari in Africa, an exciting and exotic vacation filled with wonderful memories that I treasure still.

I call this my Town and Country *shot. My friend John Reilly spent an afternoon with me creating these professional photos. It was exciting to be treated like such a star—almost like a model in the magazine!*

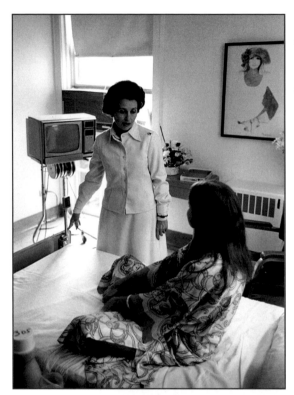

In developing Special Services for Patients at Reese, I forged a new path to create a hospital environment focused on the patient.

After Kathy was treated for kidney disease and received a transplant, I dedicated my time and efforts to the National Kidney Foundation of Illinois. My ultimate success came with the creation of the KidneyMobile, which helps screen for symptoms and save lives.

PART IV

RAISING MONEY, MAKING A DIFFERENCE

Fund-Raising 101

I tried to set a good example for my girls by doing work I saw as important. My next foray into charity work was closer to home, in Winnetka, for the Jewish Community Centers. A good part of our fund-raising came from having benefits, something that I would continue to be involved in with various charities throughout my philanthropic career. I was finding a new way to give back and make a difference—and learning and having fun at the same time.

I adopted a formula for successful fund-raising that I have used ever since. It came from Zollie Frank of Z Frank Chevrolet, one of the top car dealers in Chicago. (1) Have a good idea of how much people can contribute so you don't embarrass those who don't have much to give and (2) ask for a sum larger than you expect to receive; this gives the giver a chance to come down and get credit for being generous, and you get what you really want in a nice way. Remarkably simple and wise advice!

Adding to this formula early on, I began paying special attention to matching people and interests. I tried to interpret the passions of potential benefactors and tie those to the needs of the organization and the outcomes the project would create. In each situation, I began by

97

doing serious research to uncover *who* was interested in *what* and *why* they were interested. When I called on someone to ask for a donation, I had already done my homework and knew how to sell. Sometimes it worked; sometimes it didn't. When it didn't, I went back to find out why—and then approached it from another angle. I was determined, to say the least! And most of the time, I was successful, which, from a strictly analytical point of view, was somewhat amazing. I developed a good track record.

I had friends who told me they were embarrassed or uncomfortable to ask others for money. It didn't bother me because I was always requesting support for causes that I believed in and that were worthy recipients, and I made sure to go to people who shared similar interests and had the resources and largess to fund them. I made it about more than just the money. My friendly "people person" personality helped me to accomplish whatever I set out to do.

In addition, my experiences on the stage taught me about the "performance" aspect of fund-raising. Instead of distracting people from their fears—as a dancer or acrobat—I discovered what their individual passions were and directed them philanthropically. After that, the show went on with or without the individual patron, and I kept going as well, undeterred. I wasn't going to let anything slow me down.

Benefits That Benefit

Soon I started fund-raising on a more or less full-time basis. On any given day, I had so much fun that I didn't know what made me happier—raising my girls or raising money for charity. Both had tangible outcomes that I could see. I had a sense that I was making Chicago—and the world—a better place and trying to help my daughters become the best people they could be to contribute to that world.

Over time, I raised millions of dollars for various charities through the creation of benefit events. People say the benefits I had a hand in were unique and memorable experiences. I know my efforts, and those of the many volunteers who worked on those events, were also financially beneficial to the organizations for which they were sponsored. As I had for fund-raising, I developed a trademark tactic for producing fabulous benefits. It was simple in theory but challenging to execute. I figured out how to create an experience, and then I got someone to underwrite it.

Large parties thrown to benefit a cause were and still are a type of underground economy that operates in broad daylight and within fairly narrow socioeconomic boundaries. Without them, many of our nation's finest institutions would be unable to meet their operating expenses. They are critical to the operations of many nonprofit institutions while engaging people who might not otherwise be aware of their missions. But the process of juggling all of the people and pieces can range from demanding and exhausting to petty and even silly, and I worked to master it all. To play you need a huge Rolodex and access to the right people. Fund-raising is about whom you know, what you know, and who you are.

There is an important exchange of benefits that creates value for everyone who is involved, both the individuals and corporations who support the organizations and, obviously, the organizations themselves. It would be very nice if everyone who was able to do so would reach deep into his or her pockets to support various causes, but sometimes it takes a party to encourage people who want to give to do so. Benefits enable them to attend a party, usually on a grand scale, and experience unique entertainment. Often, they learn something about the sponsoring organization and its mission that they didn't know before. They have fun and can socialize in the company of people who are as wealthy and important as—or more than—they are.

I turned fund-raising into a sort of game for myself and invented the rules that I, and later others, would play by. I learned the ropes on my own, never afraid to assume the responsibility so that the job could be done—and done well. Because I kept raising the stakes for myself, I had to get better at researching the potential players in order to increase my chances of success. A particular triumph came as the result of mixing my fund-raising benefits and my work at Cabrini-Green and the Chicago Youth Centers, to make life better for the young people served by the institutions and give them more opportunities through a full roster of programs that would enrich their lives and make a difference.

Movies and Railroads

Although I had been denied a place on the big screen, I was still a huge fan of the movies. So, I had the idea of using one of my passions, movies, to raise money for another passion, the Chicago Youth Centers (CYC). And as an example of matchmaking in its highest form, I knew that I could get premiere movies and actual movie stars through David Wallerstein's Hollywood contacts; it was his wife, Caroline, who got me onto Cabrini's board in the first place. Before or after the movie screening, I figured that we could have a party. The board was in full support, and ticket sales were phenomenal. The idea and the execution were winners.

I arranged transportation and lodging for the stars. They were all wonderful to deal with. Because of their appearances, we got enormous publicity for the events and drew a lot of attention to the CYC. Burt Lancaster came for the Chicago premiere of *Judgment at Nuremberg*, Julie Andrews came for *Mary Poppins*, and Omar Sharif came for *Doctor Zhivago*. For a little added entertainment value, we tried to tie the theme of the event to the movie. For example, when we screened *Doctor Zhivago*, we ate Russian food and drank vodka. Even the weather cooperated—it was twenty-two degrees below zero!

BENEFIT THEIR TOPIC—Mrs. Eugene Simon, Winnetka, president of Lower North Center, largest of seven neighborhood Chicago Youth Centers, talks with Burt Lancaster, one of the stars of "Judgment at Nuremberg," whose Chicago premiere May 23 will be a C.Y.C. benefit. Lewis W. Reich of Glenview (left) is president of the

Julie Andrews, star of the movie "Mary Poppins," which premiered Wednesday night as a benefit for Chicago Youth Centers, chats with some of the guests at a post-curtain party at the Ambassador West Hotel, where she was guest of honor. From left are Mrs. Eugene Simon, Miss Andrews, Mrs. Thomas Donnelley and Mrs. Elliott Donnelley. Guests at the party had bought sponsor tickets.

MEET FILM STAR—At a reception for Omar Sharif, who plays the title role in "Doctor Zhivago," Harold M. Hansen (left), 700 Windsor Rd., Glenview, and Mrs. Eugene W. Simon, 1045 Sheridan Rd., Winnetka, chat with the star. The Shore residents are members of the Chicago Youth Centers benefit committee sponsoring the film's Midwest premiere next Thursday in the Bismarck Palace Theater. (Leonard Bass Photo)

During my work for the Chicago Youth Centers, I organized premiere movie screenings, attended by stars, to raise money. Burt Lancaster came to promote Judgment at Nuremberg, *Julie Andrews came for* Mary Poppins, *and Omar Sharif came for* Doctor Zhivago.

I was pleased that our movie-themed benefits went over so well, because later, when movies began opening at more than one theater, screening benefits became impossible. Instead, "railroad benefits" at the Donnelley estate in Lake Forest were where I focused my attention.

Elliott Donnelley, who bore an uncanny resemblance to Will Rogers, loved trains, and since he had the means to nurture that love, he installed on his property a narrow-gauge railway, complete with cars large enough to seat both children and their adult companions. The opportunity to ride on his train quickly became a hot ticket in benefit circles.

Elliott was a formidable person, as was his wife, Ann, so running those events on their property was no walk in the park, but I tried my best to adhere to their high standards. Once, I noticed that the merry-go-round I brought in had sunk into the lawn that Ann was so proud of. I nearly fainted. Another year I somehow got stuck in the middle of a disagreement between Elliott and Ann about where to place the portable toilets. I remember holding up my hands and saying, "OK! You tell me where you want me to put them!"

All Aboard for Chicago Youth Centers

[TRIBUNE Staff Photo]

It's all aboard at railroad party for Chicago Youth centers held at Lake Forest estate of Elliott Donnelley. More than 3,000 persons attended charity event.

The whistles of three model steam engine trains hit a high note for the Chicago Youth centers yesterday when more than 3,000 persons turned out for a railroad party which the agency sponsored at the Lake Forest estate of Elliott Don- nelley. Attending were Mrs. B. E. Bensinger, Mrs. Gardner Stern, Graham Aldis, and Mr. and Mrs. Frank Woods, all with grandchildren. There with their children were Mr. and Mrs. William C. Douglas and William Rentscheler. Guests were required to make a minimum contribution of $25. The Chicago Youth centers operates six facilities in the city and a summer camp at Eau Claire, Mich., and a long-weekend camping program in the winter.

The Chicago Youth Centers "railroad" benefits at Elliott Donnelley's estate were a lot of fun and a huge success!

Family Values

While I was raising money, Bud and Kathy were raising my blood pressure. Bud had lost interest in working for Maurice Lenell and took a job working for a friend of his father's in the metal business. It bored him immediately. Then he tried a stint in the utilities industry but didn't fit in there, either. Nothing seemed to stick. I tried to continue to be supportive, but when he started selling miracle roman brick, the cheap faux-brick house siding, I couldn't even bear it.

Kathy had her ups and downs. She took and passed the entrance exam for membership in Mensa and was very proud of herself, but she was bored with school and scornful of New Trier. Her artistic and creative mind craved more than it could provide. When she was a junior, a teacher called to inform me that Kathy's psychological tests revealed that she might need some psychiatry. It wasn't a surprise. I had been well aware of Kathy's potential problems from the time she was five years old. We immediately took Kathy to a therapist, but she didn't cooperate. She obviously agreed to the meeting only to satisfy us, because she didn't engage at all. It was a complete waste of time. Kathy continued to act out, dressing provocatively and offering vague explanations about her whereabouts. I didn't put anything past her—sex, drinking, or drugs.

Kathy (top) was a bit of a wild child in high school, but she was as gorgeous as ever. Here, she is shown wearing a dress of mine, which Toni (bottom) later wore, too—we all wore the same size!

Despite her Mensa membership, Kathy graduated from New Trier with a mediocre grade point average. Her applications to the Rhode Island School of Design and Pratt were rejected. So, disappointed but completely responsible for her poor performance, she took her talent and anger to Moore College of Art and Design in Philadelphia. Initially, she was enthusiastic.

Kathy graduated high school and attended Moore College of Art and Design.

Kathy's rebelliousness hadn't been a surprise or even a disappointment so much as a challenge. She was as headstrong as she was talented but so difficult. I knew she was drinking too much and making other poor choices. She seemed to pride herself on being self-determined and experimental. There was no stopping Kathy once she made up her mind.

By way of personal salvation and self-preservation, I turned my attention outward and joined the Lincoln Park Zoological Society Board and the Medical Research Institute Council (MRIC) Board at Michael Reese Hospital.

Lincoln Park Zoological Society

Lincoln Park Zoo is one of two remaining free zoos in the country, and its board members help to ensure that it stays that way. It was founded in 1868 with the gift of a pair of swans that were relocated from the menagerie in New York's Central Park. The growth of the zoo exploded in 1912 with the development of the Lion House and its Great Hall and again in 1927 with the Primate House, which became home to Bushman, one of the most famous gorillas that ever lived in captivity.

Before I got there, the board had already been instrumental in the creation of the nation's first year-round children's zoo, which opened in 1959. I was part of the effort that created the Farm-in-the-Zoo that opened in 1964. Designed to show city dwellers something of the country life, it is still a unique and evolving section of the zoo.

I joined the zoo board because I loved animals and wanted to help improve the zoo and its standing in Chicago and also because my closest friend, Betty Hirsch, insisted. "It's very social!" she told me. And for a woman like Betty, who lived to be social, that was high praise. While working on the board, Betty and I, both only children, became as close as the sisters neither of us had. She was eight years younger than me, very sophisticated, and stunningly beautiful, with big green eyes. She was perpetually tan. Like my daughter Kathy, I thought Betty had a certain sad aspect to her personality, yet, also like Kathy, she was lively, fun, and very loving.

My dear friend Betty Hirsch (later Schultz; right) convinced me to join the Lincoln Park Zoo Board. Here we're shown together with a pack of malamutes in a promotional photo.

Betty had another reason for her work on the board, beyond being a social butterfly. Her father, Walter Erman, had become a founding board member after taking a trip to Africa with the dynamic young director Marlin Perkins. Perkins was a legend. During his tenure as director (1945–1962), he made zoos an integral part of American life. Then, instead of retiring, he gained personal fame as host of the popular television program *Mutual of Omaha's Wild Kingdom*. To finance and expand the zoo during his tenure, Perkins (along with Erman) helped in the development of its first formal citizen support group, on which I proudly served, the Lincoln Park Zoological Society. When Perkins's tenure ended, the zoo's veterinarian, Lester E. Fisher, became the new director, and Barbara Carr became president. She was one of the most efficient and effective people I have ever worked with. I have never known anybody who stuck to details more than she did.

Shortly after I joined the board, the president of the board resigned, and I was encouraged by other board members to apply for the position. It was appealing since it was a paying job, especially with Bud in a transitional point in his ever-evolving "career." But Erman said, "Absolutely not! William Simon's daughter-in-law certainly should not have a job." He had known Bud's father, so that was that. The idea of paying me was demeaning as far as Erman was concerned—but I was more than welcome to work without pay. I was a little irritated to say the least, but that was the way society was structured then. Women could work hard, but their opportunities, lifestyles, and finances came from their husband. Unfortunately for me, my husband was going through our resources quickly.

The early seventies were an extremely progressive time for the zoo. The partnership between the zoological society and the Chicago Park District was a good one, wherein we raised a certain amount of money each year and the city matched it. Carr was a marvelous president, and under Fisher's administration nearly a dozen significant renovations, restorations, and new facilities were completed with our help. I was privileged to work with dynamic people such as Hope McCormick and Marshall Field to help raise more than $40 million for the zoo. Bob Pritzker made an individual contribution of $15,000, given to me during our initial fund-raising for the zoo at Field's request. Personally, I thought it was kind of paltry, but Field reminded me to be thankful because it was more than enough.

The money that we raised went toward the zoo's upkeep, including renovations to the Primate House, Small Mammal House, and Bird House. The Kroc Animal Hospital and Commissary was added, as well as the Great Ape House and many other improvements. I helmed the effort to reopen Café Brauer after massive renovations. Historically, it had been a restaurant, but when I first saw it, it was a pigeon roost—and not the type that was an actual ornithological attraction at the zoo. We cleaned it up and brought it back to its former busy and bustling life.

Throughout my tenure at the zoo, I worked as chairperson of nearly every committee. To this day, I am the longest-serving member of the zoo board as well as the oldest. I am now a Life Director and very proud of all the wonderful things we have accomplished as we rebuilt the zoo and managed to keep the admission free of charge and recognized as one of Chicago's most-loved attractions.

When you are raising money for a large cultural institution, everybody is trying to get a piece of the pie, so you have to fight for what you believe in. I always liked to focus on a specific goal. One of mine was to get new trash containers placed throughout the zoo. I was always complaining to Fisher that we were a great and fun attraction—but we didn't look like Disneyworld. The trash receptacles we had were affordable but old and unattractive. The ones I wanted were $500 each, but they were pretty spectacular—and clean. Finally, after three years of perseverance, the board agreed to pay for new trash containers. The day they were installed, we got bottle of champagne and christened a container!

As a long-serving member of the Lincoln Park Zoo Board, one of my goals was to replace the trash cans with clean, modern models. Here I'm shown celebrating with Lester Fisher (left), head of the zoo; Bob Hitchens (right of me), board member; and Ray Drymalski, chair of the board.

Building on my many successes with the zoo, I was asked to be in charge of the Zoo Ball. I knew exactly what needed to be done. The Zoo Ball was unusual in Chicago because socially it included all of the people primarily associated with supporting the Chicago Symphony, the Lyric Opera, and Ravinia, Chicago's summer musical venue in Highland Park; the zoo was the common denominator.

I initiated two changes to the ball when I started planning: time of year and place. Previously, the ball had been held in the Lion House during winter, but I felt that to increase the number of people who would attend as well enhance the experience, we had to move it into the zoo as a whole and hold it in the summer, when the guests could enjoy lovely weather and the zoo grounds in bloom. Although those changes were made, as circumstances would have it, I would not chair the Zoo Ball after all.

Another achievement at the zoo was the annual Zoo Ball. I helped turn it into an event to remember. Howard Morgan was my date; his wife had passed away, and he wanted me to show him what to do if he were to go out with someone else.

Around that time, I was set to begin a new career at Michael Reese Hospital in the fall, so I selected someone to head the ball and helped with details for it as I could. I would have loved to chair the ball, but there was no way I could do both. Eventually, Shirley Ryan, an instrumental supporter of the zoo, along with her husband, Pat, partnered with the Junior League to organize as the Women's Board of the Zoo and work in conjunction with the zoo board to plan the ball.

Michael Reese Hospital—Medical Research Institute Council (MRIC)

My work at the Medical Research Institute Council at Michael Reese Hospital was a nice complement to my involvement at the zoo. It was an equally exciting and prestigious institution. Founded in 1881, the hospital was one of the oldest and most respected hospitals in Chicago; it had a superb reputation. I had personal experience there, as well: it was the hospital I turned to for my abdominal surgery after Kathy was born.

It was the hospital that Chicago turned to when the medical situation was puzzling.

The Medical Research Institute Council of Michael Reese was renowned for groundbreaking discoveries. The Reese researchers were the first to explore the relation between coronary heart disease and cholesterol concentration in the blood, they perfected the use of the electrocardiograph, and they pioneered the development and use of the gastroscope. They also made important discoveries about the "gate-keeper" action in insulin and were the first to kill the polio virus and make an effective vaccine against it.

The Michael Reese Medical Research Hospital Board, at the time led by Lester Crown, was as serious and educational as the zoo board was social and public. I discovered that medical research is usually the easiest cause for which to raise money because it benefits everybody, both those afflicted by certain conditions and the ones who love and care for them. I stepped up my own research on any prospective donors. Quickly, I found out that most people are affected by illness in some way at some point in their lives. People who have had the devastating personal experience of serious sickness understand the issue and often are more willing to give and help.

I had some previous experience in the medical fund-raising field, when I had written letters for the Multiple Sclerosis Foundation with Renee Crown. Once I got to Reese, I learned quickly and developed a reputation in the fund-raising community for making difficult things appear easy. Putting my skills to work, I was once again able to discern the perfect match between donor and request and bring in funds to support the hospital, as well as its patients.

Meanwhile, my capacity to dance around difficulties, project stage poise and presence, smile wide, and improvise was coming in handy as my dear family experienced more difficulties.

Growing Pains

After finishing her sophomore year at Moore College, Kathy abruptly quit school and returned to Chicago. Without any conversation, she got a job at Marshall Field's in the tie department and rented an apartment on Bellevue Place in the city. She didn't tell us why she wasn't returning to school. In fact, she didn't tell us much at all. Much to my dismay, she was too busy dating her way through the society playboys to have time for her family.

Kathy's issues, demands, and secrecy began to have an effect on her sister, as did Bud's problems, ranging from his drinking, to his lingering physical problems, to his ever-evolving careers. To this day, I am very sorry that when Toni needed me for advice, comfort, and companionship, I was frequently busy and my maternal responses were most often directed at Kathy because her deviations and needs were more obvious.

And so after a decade and a half as my easy child, around sixteen, Toni found her life suddenly beginning to chip away at the values she defined herself by. She had been a wonderful cheerleader, but on her second tryouts for the varsity squad, she was passed over for political reasons. Subsequently, she became so depressed that her grades plummeted. But most devastating of all, her beloved boyfriend was stolen by a rival suitor when Toni was at summer camp.

Our family was strong and supportive, but Toni began having typical teenage boy problems that affected her usually sunny disposition.

Toni's dreams of a future that included her true love and a picket fence were shattered. And somehow with that she abandoned the notion that love and trust were achievable in relationships. She was devastated, but her emotions were understated, similar to my reaction when Alan Tishman told me about Peggy Westheimer. But for the rest of her life, Toni mourned the romantic loss and bore deep wounds and visceral scars.

The dip in her scholastic grades affected her opportunities. She didn't get into the eastern schools of her choice, so she went off to Beaver College, a small liberal arts college in Pennsylvania. She lasted only a semester, transferring to Miami of Ohio without asking or even informing us. She wasn't interested in college. She wanted to get married to the boy who had jilted her. By that time, Bud and I had sold the colonial house with the white picket fence, so that model of Toni's fantasy had also been destroyed.

With Kathy living in the city and Toni living in Ohio, Bud and I bought a California-style house on a hill in Winnetka. It was very modern, with a travertine entrance and a huge living room with a cathedral ceiling and windows on two sides overlooking the ravine. It had beach rights but only two bedrooms. It wasn't a house for raising kids; it was a house for grown-up entertaining, something I did a lot of as a fund-raiser. Before we had a chance to move into our new home, however, a series of disasters struck that made issues with the girls seem like child's play.

Crisis Comes in Fours

Bud didn't feel well—nothing dramatic—so it was a complete shock when our doctor, my cousin Eddie Elisberg, told him that he had suffered a heart attack. Bud was admitted to the hospital for lengthy observation and recovery.

While he was in the hospital, the violent pains that my friend Betty had been having became unbearable. For a long time she had claimed they were due to menopause and refused to see a doctor, but once they became excruciating, I insisted that she be evaluated. She agreed to an operation. I was sitting with her mother and father in the hospital waiting room when the surgeon came out and told us that it was ovarian cancer and Betty had a year to live.

I was devastated and tried to turn to Kathy for support, but she was as elusive as ever. She didn't visit with me. She had a million excuses, but I knew she was intentionally avoiding me, and I didn't have the strength to argue.

I was reeling from the news about Betty, worried about Bud, and frustrated by Kathy when my father, who had been in the hospital for two weeks, died suddenly. It was the only time I have ever considered backing out of a responsibility. One of the Donnelleys' railroad benefits was on my schedule, and I just didn't feel up to it. However, my mother counseled against canceling. She told me I had to do it because I was committed.

I knew she was right. Elliott Donnelley was very sympathetic. He walked me around his estate and shared his feelings about his own father's death. So despite my very agonizing personal grief, the show—as usual—went on.

After Bud recovered from his heart attack, instead of going back to selling miracle brick, he became a stockbroker. I have no idea whether he was good at it, but he seemed happy doing it, and I was happy for him. We tried to continue with life as usual.

One night we were going into town to have dinner. I told Kathy that I'd come and pick her up afterward so that she could spend the night at our house and we could visit and catch up. I had rarely seen her and was worried about her. I missed her terribly.

After dinner, Bud waited in the car as I let myself into Kathy's Bellevue apartment. I found her in bed with a guy. They were both stoned and drunk. I was furious and yelled at her to get herself together. She was woozy, but she tried. She got dressed and came home with me as I demanded but passed out in the car on the way there.

The next night, Kathy shared something that haunts me to this day.

"Mom," she said in a quiet and gentle matter-of-fact tone, "I just had a bastard."

Suddenly, I had a flash of a memory from a few months earlier. After visiting Bud in the hospital, Kathy had stopped by the house to say hello. I had taken one look at her and said, "If I didn't know better, I'd think you were pregnant." She just laughed at the time, and I was so busy that I didn't give it another thought.

I was devastated, for so many reasons. Suddenly, terribly, I realized that while my father lay dying on one floor of Michael Reese Hospital, Kathy had been giving birth on another floor at the same hospital. The date was August 11, 1965. The baby was a boy. The baby's father wanted to marry her, but she refused and gave the baby up for adoption immediately. I knew that Kathy had given my grandson away because she knew I would have done everything in my power to support her and the baby. She wanted nothing to do with it.

I was beside myself with enormous grief. However, Kathy insisted that none of it bothered her and claimed that she wanted to get pregnant only for the experience of having a baby. I was tired of Kathy's shocking behavior, and I started to cry, out of frustration, pain, and pity. I cried and continued to cry all night long. I didn't think I would ever stop crying. It hurt so much and for so many reasons. The fact that I did not know my own daughter was pregnant made me feel absent as a mother and deprived of an opportunity that so many women anticipate with such glee. She gave my grandson away for adoption, which was most likely in the best interests of the child, but it was inconceivable to me that she could be so cavalier about it. Beneath the veneer of her indifference, I knew that my child was hurting. She may have been in denial, but I was not.

Bud was as tortured as I was. Toni was simply furious with her sister. I'm sure it was because, in some measure, Toni was denied the perfect motherhood she imagined she would have with her lost love. I also would guess that it had to do with the fact that Toni suspected something was going on but, as I did, pushed it out of her mind. Toni had gone with Kathy to visit my father in the hospital when he was dying. She remembered my father saying to Kathy, "Goodness, you look great, Kathy. You got your shape back." My father acknowledged that something was different about Kathy's figure. Why didn't we notice? This was especially difficult for Toni because of her sometimes complicated relationship with her sister. Kathy froze Toni out, as well as the rest of us.

Despite the fact that Kathy outwardly projected bravado, denial, and nonchalance, she eventually fell apart. She couldn't function. She didn't feel right. She was in trouble. And she knew it. In retrospect, I think that Kathy's initial collapse was brought on by postpartum depression. Although my mother and I had both experienced a similar condition, with my mother denying it and going off to California for an extended stay and with me confronting it by returning home to study myself with Therese Benedek, neither of us initially recognized the symptoms presenting themselves in Kathy because she was so successful in covering them up. She may have done a good job of hiding the physical symptoms of pregnancy, but in the end she was incapable of masking the psychological and emotional toll.

I knew it was serious. Kathy had been suffering from emotional problems since she was a child. She had substance abuse problems. With postpartum depression added to her psychological cocktail, all hell broke loose. I called Chestnut Lodge, a private psychiatric hospital in Rockville, Maryland, that I had heard cured people with mental problems. Located twenty miles northwest of Washington, D.C., Chestnut Lodge had been operating as a private psychiatric sanitarium for the care of nervous and mental diseases since 1910. I'm not sure how I knew about the place, but I did. There was a bed there available for Kathy. It was expensive, but Bud and I were willing to do what needed to be done.

As a facility for the wealthy, Chestnut Lodge was also the dumping grounds for severely disturbed children of the seriously rich. Kathy didn't quite fit in, and her doctor wasn't a good match, either. We were assured that he was skilled and would work in Kathy's best interests. However, she was on suicide watch for the first week, which disturbed her greatly. The first report I got from the social worker included a comment about how remarkable it was that she was so orderly. I thought to myself, So what? She was always orderly. I later learned that most people who fall apart are not orderly or clean, let alone meticulously groomed. Kathy was trying to hold herself together as best she could. Leaving her there, I felt as if I was the one who might fall apart.

I used to send her jigsaw puzzles to pass the time and a million get-well cards that made her laugh.

"Are you crazy, mother?" she'd giggle.

"No, you are," I would say, jokingly. Making the painfully serious matter a little lighter seemed to do us both some good.

Bud and I went back every five weeks to visit, and she seemed to be OK. She had a room in the hospital building. When we visited, we stayed in a building named after Frieda Fromm-Reichmann. It was several awful shades of green and very upsetting. There was an heiress who followed me around like a bloodhound every time I visited. She looked more like a bag lady than an heiress in that she wore all of her clothes—every single thing she owned—at the same time. Each time I returned home, I had a headache that lasted for days. It was all so disturbing.

Back home, I decided to tackle the problem of gossip head-on. I said that Kathy had some problems and would be back when she got well. So there was no gossip because I said it out loud: "She's in a hospital for treatment." I didn't pretend.

Not that I had any time to worry about gossip. Betty was reaching the end and asked me to stay with her. I took a leave of absence from my fund-raising duties and divided my time between Kathy and Betty. Betty's disease was faster than Kathy's recovery; she succumbed to the cancer the following year at the age of only forty-two. Kathy's progress was very slow. After months of working with her dubious doctor, she told me that she felt she needed somebody different, stronger. But it was fate and not me that intervened. Her doctor got drafted.

I insisted on meeting Kathy's new doctor despite the fact that it was against the rules in those days. Adamant, I said, "I'll be dammed if I'm going to pay the ransom you charge and not meet her doctor!" Voila!

Kathy and I met with him, and I thought he was all right. As it turned out, he helped Kathy a great deal, but the pace was slower than any of us would have liked.

At the end of Kathy's first year at Chestnut Lodge, Bud and I agreed that if she didn't get well, she would have to go to a state institution. Unlike most of the other families whose loved ones were there with Kathy, we couldn't afford to keep her there forever. Beyond the cost, our prevailing concern was that the place could become a familiar "feel-good" country club retreat that she would not want to leave.

The idea of a state institution must have made an impact on her because she moved out in not quite two years, explaining (rather cryptically), "I got tired of sick people." But whatever they did there, it worked. Her reason returned and with it her confidence and ability to function. She had gone in as a vacant space, empty of herself. She came out with faith in her ability to live again.

To keep Kathy near her doctor, my good friend Buddy Mayer got her a job at the Museum for African Art in Washington, D.C., where she could commute to Rockville for appointments. While she was able to perform professionally, she continued to struggle with personal relationships.

When Toni graduated from Miami University with a degree in English, my then widowed mother, Bud, Kathy, and I attended her graduation. Toni decided to move to New York and get a job there. Not long after that, Kathy returned to Chicago and got a job cataloging Bob and Buddy Mayer's art collection. Buddy was a close friend over the years, and she supported many of the things I was involved in; now she was helping my daughter, and I was grateful. For all of Kathy's inner demons, she was so meticulous in everything she undertook that their insurer said it was the best job they had ever seen.

Toni transferred to Miami of Ohio and graduated with a degree in English (like me).

Having a Ball

With the girls' lives more under control, I was able to return to my fundraising duties. When the Medical Research Institute Council (MRIC) started having what it called the Crystal Ball to raise money for medical research, the event immediately became "the" benefit in Chicago. Only the most connected and/or experienced women were offered the chairpersonship of the council. And even though I had earned my turn by that time, having served on the board for a good number of years, I turned down the invitation to chair the ball for three years in a row. I was intimidated. Unlike other women considered for a leadership position, I didn't have a husband with the connections necessary to pull off such an event.

However, despite the ball's early successes, it wasn't growing in subsequent years. By the midsixties, attendance and enthusiasm were teetering. They continued to ask me to chair the event, and I kept saying no until finally, in 1968, I smiled and said, "I'd love to." What changed my mind? The invitation came with a challenge—it was a do-or-die proposition. They needed someone to make it better. It was my license to use my imagination and put my skills to work.

The timing was right for me. Bud had recuperated physically from his heart attack, and he was happy being a stockbroker. Kathy had recovered psychologically and was making progress both personally and professionally. Toni was in New York City looking for a job. I had my life back and a new challenge. To celebrate being back on track, our family embarked on an exciting experience that would bring us all closer together.

Africa

To celebrate my fiftieth birthday in August of 1968, Bud and I took the girls on safari in Africa. It was the trip of a lifetime and a very unique experience at the time. We were some of the first people we knew to venture to the continent to explore its vast beauty and rich treasures. Each day brought spectacular new sights and experiences that have stayed with me forever since.

En route to Africa, by way of Athens, Crete, and Rhodes, we drank champagne, ate caviar, and soaked up the Greek sunshine. Once in Nairobi, I hosted a cocktail party to allow my daughters an opportunity to meet the group of young hobby hunters who were there and among whom Bud would spend his upcoming time. Once the men took off to hunt big game, Kathy, Toni, and I spent the next three weeks sightseeing the game reserves with a driver and a guide. As luck would have it, we ended up seeing far more animals than the hunters did!

We started in the exotic seaport of Mombasa, East Africa's largest port and Kenya's main tourist hub. I was in culture shock because the locals went around without tops—and I couldn't conceive of leaving the house without a bra! I called my mother and said, "Mom, I'm on the other side of the world!"

From Mombasa we drove to Dar es Salaam in Tanzania. It had a dangerous vibe that impeded pleasure. There was an encampment of Chinese soldiers that gave the feel of a police state. It was an interesting experience, but I was terrified because no one knew whether the Chinese army was our friend!

After leaving Dar es Salaam, our first campsite was at Amboseli, Kenya. By now Americans have a classic iconic image of Amboseli captured in *National Geographic* photographs: elephant herds strolling across the plains in front of snow-capped Mt. Kilimanjaro and myriad locals working with cattle. The wildlife was fantastic. The mountain was so majestic at dawn and at sunset. The light at those times was clear and soft and magic.

Amboseli National Park offers the best opportunity for seeing a spectacular range of wildlife: lions, buffalos, cheetahs, gazelles, hyenas, jackals, wildebeests, zebras, and baboons. The black rhino, critically endangered today, was still thriving at the time. And the streams from Kilimanjaro not only serve as watering holes for the animals but also create swamps that attract and support a rich diversity of birdlife—and some pretty varied human life, as well.

It so happened that there was another group from California staying near us and we went over to visit them. As I was getting out of the hunting car, one of the men introduced himself as Dr. Robert Jampolis. I asked him whether he had ever lived in Chicago. He said he had. Did he go to the University of Chicago? "Yes," he said. I couldn't believe it. In the middle of the African bush, I saw someone with whom I had gone to college!

From Amboseli, the girls and I traveled back to Tanzania to the world's largest intact collapsed volcano, the Ngorongoro Crater. We got there at the end of the day, and the sunset was stunning. The girls were tired, but I went out to take photographs and bumped into a German man dressed in lederhosen who was also taking pictures. He turned out to be an architect and was in Africa to redo the lodge manager's house. He asked me to join him for a drink, and I said that would be lovely but told him that he would have to invite my daughters and guide as well. He obliged.

After cocktails the first night, the German architect invited me and the girls to dinner the next night for his special Hungarian goulash. When we arrived, there was goulash, along with candles, flowers, and music. This wasn't dinner; it was foreplay! After our meal, I politely extracted myself and the girls, and he was quite frosty. I didn't realize that he expected me to stay, until he got upset with me when I thanked him and went home. Still, it was a fun experience. The food was fabulous. The music was wonderful. And he was a great big, attractive, and smart man. It was flattering.

The next morning, we went with the guide down into the crater and saw flamingos, rhinoceroses, wildebeests, and zebras. The entire area was so rich in history and beauty that everywhere we looked was something breathtaking and ancient.

Eventually, we made our way to Bill Holden's place, known as Mount Kenya Safari Club. It was unbelievably elegant. Located high on the slopes of Africa's second-highest mountain, the complex straddled the equator in a glorious assortment of luxurious cottages and elegant buildings set amid manicured lawns and decorative ponds. Ever since the club was founded in 1959 by the late film star, it served as a mecca for the international jet set, royalty, aristocracy, and the rich and famous. There were peacocks strolling around, and a baby cheetah licked the girls' hands.

During our trip to Africa, every day was like a scene out of a Stewart Granger movie!

After our luxurious adventure, we journeyed to a tented camp in Seronera. Bud called us there and invited us to join him in Nairobi, which was too far away to drive, so a four-seat plane was sent to pick us up. Flying over the Rift Valley in the late afternoon was one of the most thrilling and exciting things I've ever done. Ribbons of animals were migrating beneath us, just like in the movie *Out of Africa*. Upon landing, a triumphant and glowing Bud was there to greet us. His hair had grown long, and he looked so gorgeous. I told him, "You have to keep it that way," and he said, "I'll do that if you stop wearing a panty girdle"—and I never wore one after that.

Although Bud had been hunting elephants, he shot and killed a buffalo, a lion, four antelopes, a gazelle, and a few zebras. Caught up in the "when in Rome" mentality, Kathy decided that she was up for the hunt as well. She not only went out to shoot with her father but also shot better than he did. "I couldn't stand to see them suffer," she said, "so I had to do it with one shot."

Bud enjoyed hunting while in Africa and was quite successful. He shot this eland and other big-game animals.

Not to be outdone by her father, Kathy proved to be a skilled huntress as well.

We flew from Cyprus to Cairo and had six hours there. I had arranged for a guide. No Jews were allowed in at the time, but we took our chances. We rode camels, saw the Sphinx up close, and went to the pyramids. The next day we could hardly walk, as the steps were so steep!

From Cairo we went to Israel with a wonderful guide, a Palestinian who was the guide for Danny Kaye. We saw the whole state of Israel: Jerusalem, Tel Aviv, Haifa. The Golan Heights amazed me; they looked like a hill in Wisconsin. We saw the prison at Acre and spent Yom Kippur in Tel Aviv. We went to Bethlehem, which was very commercial. We also saw the Wailing Wall in Jerusalem and all the famous mosques and temples.

From Israel we went to Sienna, where our first European guide met us. He had a 1938 touring car and drove us all over with the top down. There was a Middle Ages festival going on, and we had such fun enjoying it all. He then took us to Florence, where we saw the Uffizi Museum and *David* and toured the lovely city. The girls went on to London and then home. Bud had left us in Israel, and I flew home from Florence.

What a trip—I still marvel. It was the most fantastic, exotic experience that nine weeks can offer. It was all first class, and I look back on it with memories that fill my heart with joy and wonder.

Farm Life

Back from Africa, I returned to my duties planning for the Crystal Ball while Bud decided that his next career would be one that brought him closer to the earth. The lure of the African wild must have worn off on him! Being a stockbroker had lost its allure, and he suddenly became passionate about the idea of himself as a weekend gentleman farmer.

A farmhouse and barn up the hill from Bud's family home had come up for sale—seventy-five acres of Wisconsin farmland overlooking a large lake for only $50,000. Bud was thrilled. By this time, the "gentleman farmer" was somewhat cash poor, however, and so the down payment of $10,000 came from my mother.

We closed on the farm on July 20, 1969, the same day that Neil Armstrong walked on the moon. We may as well have, too, for all that we knew about farming. Still, at first, I was optimistic about this new, starkly different chapter of our life. I began cleaning and redecorating. I got started scrubbing and then redid the bathroom and kitchen and furnished the house. We also put up a new fence as we settled in. I started to imagine getting a cow and some chickens.

In the beginning, the weekends on the farm were great and restful. We walked, picked raspberries, grew watercress, bought corn, and planted flowers. Because they were much closer, we spent more time with Bud's family. No matter how difficult Bud's mother was, I loved his family as my own. I didn't have a lot of family nearby, as my cousins were strewn all over the world, so the Simons were my family, and they were marvelous to me.

Bud's next life stage led us to weekends on our farm in Wisconsin. This gorgeous quarter horse was his favorite girl.

Eventually, as usual, Bud began itching for change and getting grander ideas about farming. Ranchers need horses, so he started with the purchase of a quarter horse. Once he had a horse and property to roam, he needed cattle. Bud couldn't buy just any cattle; he wanted exotic cattle. Excited for his new venture, he went to Missouri to buy expensive and unusual Charolais cattle. I was not, however, as enamored as were the breeders and my husband.

When they arrived by truck, it was really a shock. First of all, I didn't know that cows were so different from each other. They each got out of the truck in their own way. Some got out like ballet dancers, some fell out, some wouldn't get out at all, some backed out, and some jumped out headfirst. The sight was bizarre. I had thought that Bud went to Missouri to buy a couple of cows, but they just kept coming—forty in all.

Herding cattle—while wearing a hat and smoking a Marlboro on a quarter horse—was pretty much the extent of Bud's interest. Caring for the pricy beasts was another matter. We had to find somebody who knew how to take care of them, and they weren't the kind of cows that other people had, so it wasn't easy. Finally, Bud hired a man and his wife to live in our farmhouse in order to take care of the cattle every day. Needless to say, money was flying out of our pockets to care for cows. In Wisconsin, the cows there were milking cows and Black Angus. The difference in value was enormous, and I had expected at most two cows. Luckily, I was soon able to turn my attention away from the cows and back to my girls, as well as myself—and my responsibilities planning the Crystal Ball.

Back to the Ball

There are thousands of decisions, big and small, that go into an event. Everything must be considered: where to stage it, who the entertainment will be, what's included in the goody bag. A benefit that is beautiful, elegant, entertaining, original, celebrity studded, and successful—one that sparkles—relies on 95 percent of the decisions being "right."

Today, there are written histories from other balls to use as a guide, but back then I was winging it. I knew from experience that big problems occurred when the selection of coworkers was careless. Because the finances as well as the details are enormous, many people select a cochair to share the responsibility and burdens of a huge event. This often leads to arguments and ego wars. To avoid that, I decided instead to select a vice chair. The woman I selected was rumored to be a good fund-raiser because her husband was very well connected. Yet, she was upset that she was not officially named a "cochair," and this inequity festered throughout our tenure. This especially irked me because she had initially accepted vice chairmanship without qualms and then only later began to change her behavior.

My second-biggest mistake was agreeing to allow a professional party planner to head the decorating committee. She was certainly qualified to do so, but as it turned out, she didn't work well with others. She refused to hold or attend meetings and engage other volunteers, all the while seeking adulation and appreciation for what she did individually and ineffectually. Suffice it to say that the education that came from the Crystal Ball was invaluable in terms of what I learned about managing volunteers.

For a fresh chance of pace, I decided to hold the event at Chicago's historic and venerated Palmer House. Having opened its doors in 1871—nearly two weeks before the Great Chicago Fire—and burned to the ground once already, I figured nothing as bad as that was likely to happen again. Also, my former dancing teacher, Muriel Abbott, had hired all the shows for the Palmer House and heartily endorsed it. The place was always active, fun, and alive—the perfect setting for our occasion.

I have always believed in the power of a star to draw crowds, so I hired Barbra Streisand's half sister, Roslyn Kind, to perform. Her voice was similar, but she was available and Barbara was not. At any rate, I was sure that I was discovering another star—she was so pretty! On a trip to Colorado, I met her for an interview and was instantly charmed. With the talent secured, I was on my way to a memorable ball.

Once the committees, the venue, and the star were set, my concerns became personal. The chair of the Crystal Ball can't wear just anything! I flew to New York to look at a selection of dresses. After playing endless dress up, I was invited to lunch at Côte Basque by Jerrie Rosenberg, the famous buyer for Bonwit Teller.

I mentioned that my daughter was living in New York, so she told me to bring her along. Toni was cute and charming, as always, and Jerrie asked her what her plans were. Toni admitted that she didn't really have any, so Jerrie arranged for her to meet Peggy Kaufman, who was in charge of public relations and fashion shows for Bonwit's. Peggy hired Toni on the spot, and they became good friends. When she eventually returned to Chicago, Toni was in charge of Yves St. Laurent's upscale boutique, Rive Gauche.

RIVE GAUCHE IN CHICAGO: When St. Laurent's boutique opens in Bonwit Teller in Chicago Feb. 27, 24-year-old Toni Simon will be in charge. She's just spent a week at Rive Gauche New York learning all about the clothes and how they're worn. "We're going to buy fashion and show it. At least 50 per cent of the stock will be in the new long lengths." Toni doesn't have any Longuettes in her wardrobe yet, but soon will. "I think it's really fun. I always thought the longer lengths were for tall, slender people. But they're right for every woman, if worn correctly. I think American women are ready for change. But I think the short skirts will hang on. Women will wear what they want, like they did last fall." What Toni likes to wear are simple, elegant clothes. Her favorite at Rive Gauche is the fitted caraco blouse, with muttonchop sleeves and a ruffle at the waist, worn over a Midi skirt.

Toni Simon

After living in New York and working with Peggy Kaufman at Bonwit Teller, Toni came back to Chicago and was the head of Yves St. Laurent's Rive Gauche boutique.

Things were moving along nicely. I began to imagine possible improvements in the format of the Crystal Ball. I started with cocktails. In the past, the Crystal Ball had always charged for drinks before dinner, and I didn't like that one bit. I thought, "How can you charge for drinks at a fancy affair like this?" It was awkward. I was told I needed to raise $50,000 to have gratis drinks.

Nancy Greenebaum, the wife of my old college flame Bob, told me that her brother-in-law Edger was willing to help with the event. So I called him, and he gave me ten grand to sponsor the drinks. From there I got eight MRIC board members to give me five grand each, so I had fifty thousand to underwrite the cocktails. Ta-dah! Now, that was an improvement!

Then just as one problem was solved, another arose. The Jewish Federation was planning on holding its fiftieth-anniversary benefit the same night. A lot of people were putting pressure on me to change my date because it "belonged" to someone else. We had a board meeting and then another and another, all discussing the ramifications to our attendance. Finally, I pled my case: "All right, look: we can't do anything about it. They are having an event, and we are having an event. We have to do the best we can." That settled the matter, and we both kept our dates and hoped for the best.

Nips and Tucks

Another matter was being settled by Kathy: she had met a man and had fallen in love. Steve Poster was at Gamma Photo Labs looking out the window when he saw Kathy walking down the street and ran outside to meet her. They hit it off. He had been born and raised in Chicago and worked as a still photographer but wanted to break into the film industry. He was so poor at the time that he didn't even own a car, but Kathy was charmed by him.

I asked Kathy what she saw in him, and she said that he made her laugh. He did not make me laugh, however—especially after he moved into Kathy's room with her in our house in Winnetka. He had nothing of his own, but they planned to live together, which irked me. This was before so many young people were beginning to live together, so I was less open to the idea. But this was Kathy. She loved risk and drama.

At the time, I, too, had been toying with a little risk and drama of my own. I was standing in my father's coat factory, looking at my reflection, and I thought, "I don't look the way I want to look." Specifically, I didn't like the lines running from the corners of my mouth to the bottom of my face. I decided to do something about it and began interviewing plastic surgeons. I talked to three in Chicago and one in New York and settled on Dr. Tom Rees in Manhattan.

The girls in Dr. Rees's office were beautiful. He looked like James Coburn and was the nicest man. During our consultation, he encouraged me to move forward with the procedure and confirmed that I was the perfect age for it to make the maximum impact. He said he would do his own wife's face when she got to be my age. I trusted his assessment and scheduled the face-lift.

My house was crowded with Kathy and Steve, so I was happy to have a reason to get out of town for a while—especially once Bud insisted that if they were going to live together, they had to get married. They agreed to his request. Kathy didn't want a big wedding, and I didn't argue. I think the fact that we let her marry him, let alone insisted on it, was crazy. The whole thing didn't sit well with me. I told Steve that Kathy was addictive and begged him not to let her get involved with drugs.

My stress level was already high when I got to New York and checked into a small hotel on 80th Street in Manhattan. Once there, my panic deepened. I remember looking out the window at the November snow and thinking, "What am I doing? This is my face!" It was one month before the Crystal Ball, and I was going to be wearing my hair up. I couldn't risk any medical mishaps.

By the morning of the surgery, I had calmed down. I remember Dr. Rees saying, "OK, honey, here we go." And then I woke up. The hard part had begun. I had a nurse who was so dear; she kept icing my eyes and warming my heart with soft strokes on my arm. When Toni came to see me, she told them to pull back on my medicine since I reacted so strongly I kept passing out.

After twenty-four hours in the hospital, I returned to my hotel to heal. Nobody should believe that a face-lift doesn't hurt. It hurts like hell! When I had gotten through the pain and was well enough to walk around the city, I stopped in a drug store, where the counter girl suggested I try vitamin E. It helped immensely with the healing.

Two weeks later, I had no bruising around the eyes and was stunned when I saw my before picture. The doctor had done something new at the time and lifted the muscles under the skin as well as the skin. That's why it has held for more than forty years. When I got back to Chicago, nobody knew I had had a face-lift. Everyone just thought I looked especially rested from a little time off!

With the Crystal Ball around the corner, I started paying more attention to my looks and wasn't satisfied with what I saw in the mirror. I went to New York for a face-lift, and the results were stunning—but subtle. Everyone thought I had had a restful vacation!

I had barely fully healed when Kathy married Steve. During the ceremony, it was impossible to ignore how stoned he was. I knew my admonition about her addictive personality had fallen on deaf ears and was concerned that this was going to end badly.

Kathy married Steve Poster in an small ceremony at our home in Winnetka. I had my doubts, but she seemed happy.

Bud and I gave the newlyweds money for a honeymoon in Morocco. When they returned to Chicago, they got an apartment on Seminary west of Halsted Street. It wasn't a good neighborhood in 1969. We were not happy about the location, but Kathy made that little apartment her own. I took my mother to see it before she had finished decorating, and we were both stopped cold in the bedroom. The walls were painted red, but there was no bed. "Where will they sleep?" she asked me.

"They'll sleep standing up," I joked, but I wasn't laughing. I was so sick of Kathy's stunts that it really would have been fine with me if they slept hanging from the ceiling like bats.

Bud's mother, Celeste, gave Steve enough money to join the photographer's union. For a while he filmed commercials and documentaries in Chicago, but eventually, he followed his dream and went to California. A man I had gone to school with named Bob Gottschalk, who had developed Panavision, got Steve into the union there. He worked on *Close Encounters of the Third Kind* with Steven Spielberg and on *Blade Runner* with Ridley Scott. But I knew that none of that Los Angeles scene and film business environment was good for Kathy.

The Crystal Ball

I tried to put aside my worries about Kathy and her new life, as finally, all my hard work with the Crystal Ball was about to pay off. The ball, themed "A Walk on the Moon," was held on December 5, 1969. By all accounts, it was an artistic and philanthropic success.

One thousand guests, dressed in tuxes and tulle, landed weightlessly, paraded through the entrance of the hotel, posed for photos, and plucked their crystal key chain table assignments from a replica of the moon. Lit by a series of light sources to enhance the feeling of walking on the lunar landscape, the otherworldly aspects gave way to a party to suit every taste.

For the sedate we had cocktails in the quiet elegance of the Red Lacquer Room. In the main ballroom, David LeWinter and a string orchestra performed. Bandleader Dick Judson went wild in the State Ballroom for the energetic younger group. Roslyn Kind was the main event, and she did not disappoint.

I wore a beautiful pink satin beaded dress from Bonwit's. My proudest moment was when I dedicated the event to Betty, who normally would have been at my side the whole time. I missed her dearly, and the festivities just weren't the same without her.

When all of the checks were in and the bills were paid, I had achieved my goal to raise more than a million dollars. I estimated that we lost about a hundred people to the Jewish Federation benefit. I don't know how many they lost to us. The bottom line was that we each did well. I was proud of my success but ready to pass the planning to the next chair.

New Rules

Alice Pfaelzer was chosen as my successor for the Crystal Ball. She selected my friend Sally Berger as cochair. Sally's husband, Miles, was a wealthy and well-known real estate developer. Between the two of them, they knew just about everyone who had money to give in Chicago, and I knew they'd do well.

To bring Sally up to speed, I spent one hour on the phone with her every night for a year. Refining the art of persuading people to part with large sums of money takes strategizing. We often used a method familiar to most police departments: the good cop/bad cop routine. We both would make the calls; one was very serious while the other was sweet and accommodating. Using that approach, I stressed the importance of going to corporations for money early in the season when they were making plans for the year.

As it turned out, Sally hit a snafu while working with Roy Pesch, the president of Michael Reese. He expected one of her donors to provide money for a new emergency room instead of the Crystal Ball. To smooth things out, I called Roy and invited him to my home for drinks. Although I had been working for the hospital on the board for years and lived a few driveways away from him in Winnetka, I hardly knew him at the time.

Once he arrived and the pleasantries were out of the way, I got down to business. I told him that if he didn't calm down, Sally would quit. I went on to say that I thought he should make peace with her. He listened to me and called Sally the next day to tell her that he wanted her to raise a million dollars. He promised to help her in every way he could and even gave her a car and a driver so that she could make more personal calls. Sally stayed. Through her husband she called on a huge array of contacts that included the mayor of the city and a variety of top business leaders. But the day that changed fund-raising forever for Michael Reese Hospital was when Sally met with a rough-talking guy from the Amalgamated Meat Cutters Union.

"I don't know what you ladies are doin'," he told her, "but we raise the money first and celebrate it the night of the event!"

What sweet and simple wisdom. From that day forward, we changed how we viewed our fund-raising process. Before, the common practice was to hold the event and raise the money through the event. With this change in thinking, we started to raise money to underwrite the event, and then we celebrated the night of the event and made more money helping others celebrate our success. We began also to go only to the top, to the CEOs, for money, and we got the events paid for in full first.

It was also around that time that I learned another important lesson about fund-raising in corporations and foundations. I made a personal call with Sally to somebody I'd known since kindergarten. When he handed her a check for a thousand dollars on the spot, I reminded him that when I did the Crystal Ball the year before, he didn't give me any money. "You sent me a letter," he replied. "I threw it in the wastebasket."

I learned that in addition to raising the money up front and celebrating the night of the event, the personal approach makes all the difference in whether you are going to get that money up front or ever.

The Beginning of the End

As I was learning valuable professional lessons, Bud was learning personal ones. As I predicted, he had grown weary of his Marlboro Man incarnation and decided to sell the cattle. Unfortunately, he stubbornly insisted that we hold the sale at the farm in Wisconsin, a place where people understand the value of only Herefords and Black Angus. I knew it was going to be a disaster.

We learned that the formula for selling cattle was to have a large breakfast with plenty of liquor before the sale. On this day, Bud arranged for a refreshment truck, which was late. The weather was very cold and gloomy. The morning of the sale, my housekeeper and I went into town and bought every sweet roll they had to keep people fed while they shopped. But hot coffee and donuts didn't help buyers understand why those cows cost so much.

They bid lightly, and they bid low. In the end, the buyers practically stole the few cattle they bought, and we were stuck with the rest of them whether we wanted them or not. It's not as if you can give your cattle to the anticruelty society when you don't want them anymore! The entire ordeal was both financially draining and emotionally upsetting. We should have stopped the sale before it started.

The stress it created was nearly unmanageable—so much so that Bud had his second heart attack during this time. It was major. His doctor said that he should have a heart bypass, a relatively new procedure in 1972, and Bud agreed to the surgery. He went to a hospital in Milwaukee for the operation, which turned out to be long and difficult.

During the surgery Bud developed a bleeding problem, and when it was finally over, we were told that he would have trouble recovering because he had been under anesthesia for so long.

As it turned out, "trouble" was an understatement. First, Bud was confused and paranoid. He somehow became convinced that they put his heart back in the wrong place. He obsessed over it continually. But his mental problems were only part of it. Physically, he wasn't healing. The huge wound in his chest remained open for six long months. All during that time I was responsible for washing the incision and changing his bandages. The combination of mental and physical sickness left Bud so depressed and off-kilter that once we got home, his only activity was pacing around our basement. Not only was I worn out but also we were on thin ice financially.

To eliminate some of our day-to-day responsibilities, as well as our financial burdens, I decided to put an end to the cow business. With Bud's blessing, I called the breeder in Missouri and managed to sell back to him what was left of his herd. After that, I relocated the farm manager and his wife out of our house in Wisconsin and rented it to the daughter of one of our friends on the lake.

We took a trip to Sarasota, Florida, in hopes of raising our spirits. However, we weren't given our usual good room and were plagued with bad weather, so by the time we returned home, our spirits weren't all that much better after all. Bud withdrew further. I started looking for psychiatric care again—this time for him. I found a psychiatrist at Michael Reese who prescribed mood elevators for Bud. However, after several months of talk and pills, he was still withdrawn and had taken up smoking again.

Things had gotten so low that after taking stock of our fiscal situation, I realized that I was going to need to get the first paying job of my life. I was nearly fifty-five years old. At the time, this was incongruous to someone of my generation and socioeconomic group, but I took it in stride. I could no longer afford to sit back and be nonplussed. Although I wouldn't have identified with the feminist movement at the time, as it turned out I was a pioneer feminist of sorts and, I think, a pretty good role model.

A New Phase

In the early seventies, women were just beginning to use their volunteer experiences to earn money. Kathy, who was working as a designer, and Toni, who had started a career in nursing, both were making their own money and repeatedly told me to "stop giving it away." I was enthusiastic at the prospect of earning a living, but as one of the first women I knew to translate fund-raising skills into fund-earning skills, I barely knew where to begin. Plus, I had to do it at an age when many women were retiring from volunteer work.

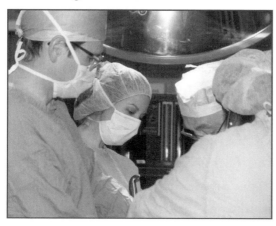

Toni worked as a surgical nurse in many hospitals throughout the city, including Northwestern Memorial and Rush Presbyterian. Doctors lauded her careful work.

I stared by going to Barat College and learning how to compose a CV. Then, partially to save face and partially to motivate myself, I practiced making the decision sound like something fun to do: a midlife adventure, personal empowerment, growth. My pride nearly got the best of me, and I couldn't bear the idea of telling people that I needed the money—particularly because Bud and I had once had so much. But I didn't have time to wallow in my problem. I had to solve it. Fast.

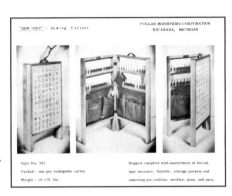

At one point, I got ambitious and went into business for myself. I developed an organizer for sewers to use to store their supplies that would fit nicely in a closet. Unfortunately, by the time my prototypes were made, sewing had fallen out of fashion. I still think it was an exciting idea!

I began by networking—way before it became commonplace for women to do so and way after men had perfected the art. Once I had a résumé, I began to talk about it whenever I had the opportunity. Rather than sending it out indiscriminately to people I didn't know, I wanted to target people who might be interested in what I had to offer. As an explanation, I'd chirp with a smile, "I'm going to work!" After people stopped looking at me as if I'd lost my mind, they started offering me jobs.

The first offer came from Clarine Hall, a woman I had worked with to build the Winnetka Children's Fair, about twenty-five years previously. She was then head of the YWCA office in Des Plaines and offered me a job as office manager. Although I told her that I didn't want to do that kind of work, she held the position open for me for three full months while I kept looking. The emotional boost was marvelous.

The second offer came from real estate magnate Leonard Richman. The job was catering manager for his prestigious Ambassador Hotel.

I appreciated his asking, but I didn't want that job, either. He also asked me to be the manager of a retirement home in Evanston, but that was about as far away as the moon from what I wanted to be doing!

In the meantime, Elliot Epstein, brother of mayoral candidate Bernard Epstein, hired me for a freelance job as an event organizer. Elliot had served on the Chicago Youth Centers with me, and he needed someone to organize a benefit featuring Groucho Marx for Governor Dan Walker. I arranged for it to be held in the Auditorium Theater, but Groucho had a stroke before we could send out the invitations, so the event was canceled. It didn't go off as planned, but it was still my first paying job!

A few weeks later, at a press party that Michael Reese Hospital was holding for Sally Berger (who was by then doing tremendously well raising money for the hospital), I told hospital President Roy Pesch about my new career path. In a surprising show of support, he gave me a job offer. I accepted. It was a perfect fit, after all. I had been raising money for Reese's medical research for more than a decade and had many experiences there both personally and professionally.

Sharing with me a novel idea that patients should be treated like human beings, he asked me, "How would you like to come and humanize the hospital?" After one conversation, I agreed that I had just what the hospital needed. But I wondered out loud how I would get all the way to the hospital in Hyde Park from my house on the North Shore. Roy said he could arrange for a car to meet me at the train station. I was so thankful for the convenience.

I still had one last concern. Despite my need for a job and genuine interest in, concern for, and history with the hospital, I knew how counterproductive hierarchies could be. I told him I'd take the job only if I could report directly to him. I have to admit it was a smart move on my part. I knew that reporting to him would give me more authority. He accepted my terms. My salary was $20,000 a year—a fraction of what my friends' husbands made but $20,000 a year more than any of my friends made.

At fifty-five, I started my first full-time paying job, as a patient advocate representative at Michael Reese Hospital. My directive was to "humanize the hospital."

Humanizing the Hospital

My job at Reese turned out to be a fantastic adventure in human psychology with heroes and villains to spare. Initially, I had no job description other than the instruction to "humanize the hospital," but I somehow instinctively knew what had to be done. In creating my new department, Special Services for Patients at Reese (SSPR), I began the process by meeting people to talk. I made appointments with the heads of each department, and I was not warmly received to say the least. Although reporting to the president, having an established relationship with the board of trustees, and knowing many of the volunteers were all empowering, my experience turned out to be a double-edged sword. The nurses thought I was a spy. The volunteers felt threatened, as did even some of the hospital's leadership. The head of social work refused to talk to me for my entire first year. I had to prove myself throughout the entire hospital, each and every day.

I decided to start humanizing Reese with the group that escorted patients from place to place in wheelchairs. They were often terribly impolite to the patients. They may as well have been transporting cattle (not Bud's precious bovines, of course, but ordinary cattle). In the process of changing their demeanor, I catered to their neglected egos by having their office painted and creating a small area for them to rest comfortably, relax, and have meals. My friend Sharon Harris designed new uniforms for them pro bono. Then I proceeded to teach them basic things, such as how to talk to patients and how to walk politely with them. I made them understand that under no circumstances could they leave a patient alone on a gurney and walk away.

To make sure they got the idea, we used role-playing. I put them on gurneys and left them alone. They got the message. We then practiced different ways of safely helping someone in and out of a wheelchair. They quickly became extremely responsive and involved. When their behavior changed, I had their titles changed to reflect their new job description more accurately. As "patient escorts" they felt cared for and important and effectively demonstrated both qualities when delivering patients throughout the hospital.

Then I turned my attention to creating a warm and welcoming respite for both patients and visitors. While visiting with Cindy Pritzker, I discussed with her the possibility of underwriting a "Marcus Welby" conservatory on the roof of the building, where a peaceful environment filled with nature and beauty would create a unique sanctuary. Cindy loved flowers and was intrigued. Unfortunately, due to constraints with the age of the building and its elevators, the project never came to fruition, but I believe it would have been a nice addition to my patient-centered program.

From there I helped reinvigorate the emergency room and the ministry and began to hire a staff. By starting a patient-centered program in Chicago, we were known as pioneers. These were the early days of actually focusing on patient care, something that has now become such an important goal and "hot topic" in health care. At that time, however, I had no job description, no model to follow. I had to prove myself through my work and my word. I developed the program on my own, seeking input from my fellow colleagues, as well as patients, as I went along. Soon, patient representatives were suddenly popping up all over the country as the collective consciousness regarding care was changing for the better. I loved being part of the sea change.

I built a strong and supportive staff and learned as much about personal psychology as I did about patient advocacy. We all wanted to make the hospital a better place for patients.

In my role at Reese, I worked to develop strong relationships with everyone at the hospital, from volunteers and heads of departments to nurses and doctors. Dr. Richard Bendix became a good friend and trusted colleague.

Children's Memorial Hospital called and invited me to meet with top administrators to discuss how they could create a patient representative program like mine. Standing before a slew of doctors, I was nervous but must have explained it well enough because Children's Memorial started a patient representative department and hired a friend of mine, Nancy Wachs, to run it. Nancy stayed on and eventually became vice president of the hospital, as well as Maggie Daly's assistant in her after-school program, After School Matters. I also helped develop programs at Rush-Presbyterian-St. Luke's, Northwestern Memorial Hospital, the University of Chicago Hospitals, and Christ Community Hospital.

The intensity of my work fostered a necessarily close relationship with Roy Pesch, the president of Reese. He became a good friend as well as a mentor. Because of our jobs, we spent a good portion of time together, but when Bud became jealous, I was surprised. Over the past five decades I had remained very close friends with my old heartbreak, Alan Tishman, and Bud never thought a thing about it.

In fact, whenever I was in New York, I would see Alan for breakfast or lunch, and I was always excited when he came to Chicago. By the time I was working at the hospital, Tish was on the board of Mount Sinai Hospital in New York and was so proud of what I had done at Reese that he wanted to use my program there. He had been a nice young man and grew into a nice old man. I almost had an affair with him once but didn't go through with it. It was during a period when I once remember thinking, "Everybody's doing it!" But I held back. Still, the attachment to Tish was nice. It was like *The Bridges of Madison County* without the sex.

Bud's instincts were good ones, however. As we grew closer, Roy and I were developing an emotionally intimate bond. Unfortunately, he was often unstable, at times extremely creative and intelligent but also an unpredictable risk taker. In my second year, he was fired. I knew then that not only was I losing someone I was fond of but also it would surely impact my influence in the hospital. But I knew the work I was doing was important, and, as always, the show had to go on.

Luckily, by the time Larry Klainer came in as the new president of Reese, I had assembled a department of eleven people and had taught other hospitals how to replicate the system. I had begun to build a reputation and had a track record and expectations to uphold.

Yet, I knew there would be changes for me, and they started with the loss of the car that drove me to and picked me up from the downtown Chicago train station. The new administration gave me money to hire a retired taxi driver to perform the same service, but after that, the taxi driver was replaced with a shuttle bus because there were so many young doctors coming from the suburbs along with me. As small as this sounds, after a life of discipline, commuting from Winnetka to Hyde Park was one of the most regimented things I'd ever done.

Klainer made many more substantive changes as well. He changed our department's goals and taught me management by objectives. I learned a lot from him. But with all of his new missions and with medical malpractice lawsuits rising across the country, the Hippocratic oath of doctors to "first do no harm" was increasingly interpreted as "do no harm to the hospital." As much as we tried to stem the tide of liability, outlines and goals are very difficult to accomplish when dealing with human feelings.

I thought I had learned all of my lessons about working with people while I navigated the benefit scene and was careful whom I hired, but I made one big mistake. She was a bright young woman with a master's degree in history and a fresh, innocent face. I was embarrassed that I had never finished my graduate work, and that insecurity came back to haunt me. Technically, my new hire did a good job and the doctors loved her, but she wanted my job and stabbed me in the back while trying to get it.

When I was in Japan at an international hospital congress, the young woman sent a letter to Reese's president, who at that point was Robert Buchanan, telling him that I was doing a terrible job and should be fired. I was shocked when I found out. She never appeared anything but sweet and competent to my face. I was told by someone in confidence, so I couldn't even address it openly. Instead, I'd go home on weekends and sob.

As it turned out, Buchanan thought highly of me and ignored the letter, but the young woman never stopped trying to undermine me. Finally, after about five months, which was a long time to endure her backhanded and despicable techniques, she quit and went to Rush-Presbyterian-St. Luke's, where she went after my counterpart's job and got it. After she left Reese, I learned that all of my staff had been wary of her and were delighted now that she was gone. I was happy to get back to my work, with a little less drama.

Timeless

During the years of going to meetings in other cities on behalf of Reese, I continued my work at the Lincoln Park Zoo and kept my ears open to what other zoos were doing. One year, I discovered a sculptor who could produce works of art that children could climb on. It was complete serendipity: I was at a patient representatives convention in Detroit, where a speaker told us about a teacher who had died unexpectedly. In memoriam, an amazing sculpture in the shape of an open heart was installed at the entrance to the teacher's school. The children were climbing in and out of it continually. I wondered whether this sculptor could do something for the zoo that would involve kids and made it my business to find out.

The sculptor, David Rodgers, lived in Bloomington, Indiana. I called and asked him whether he could do something that kids could be part of at the zoo. His response was the creation of the *Sunform*, a durable and fully functional sculptural sundial, made out of Indiana limestone. I presented his drawings at a board meeting for approval. Despite some early misgivings by prominent members, many on the board were more than interested. In fact, they were so passionate they gave me the go-ahead to have the artist start work on the sculpture.

I flew to Bloomington to see the limestone that would be used for the sculpture and examine how Rodgers would script it to tell the time of day in the a.m. on the left and the p.m. on the right. It was a fascinating concept and a great visit. The sculptor said he could create it for $25,000. I told him to begin and promised to find the money.

Board member Hope McCormick told me that Citicorp was opening an office in Chicago and suggested that the company would probably like to have its name on something public for advertising purposes. So she invited Howard Morgan, head of Citicorp in Chicago, to lunch to tell him about the project. He not only agreed to pay for it (through Citicorp) but also joined the zoo board and eventually became chairman.

The beautiful and functional sculpture was placed in Center Plaza South, opposite Park Place Café, and children have been climbing it for decades. The Indiana limestone has held up beautifully, and the smooth shape sits serenely in its surroundings.

I helped bring to Lincoln Park Zoo the popular Sunform *sculpture. Here I am shown with Lester Fisher, head of the zoo (right), and Howard Morgan (left), of Citicorp, who provided funding for the work of art and later became chairman of the zoo board.*

Breaking up with Bud

After a few years of working at the hospital, I found that the commute from Winnetka had become untenable, even with the shuttle program in place. Worse still was that Bud's problem with alcohol was not getting any better and I was sick of it. I had always said that I wouldn't bother him or pester him about his drinking, but after a few years of working hard and coming home late to find him just waking up from a nap, I was at my breaking point. One evening when we were sitting in the family room and he said, "I've made up my mind to make some changes."

I responded, "Oh, really?"

He described his plans to retire, sell the house, let the housekeeper go, resign from Lake Shore Country Club, and buy a smaller home. Where was I in this grand scheme? "You will continue to work," he said.

At that moment I made up my mind. I said, "No, I'm not going to do that," and decided to move into the city. I wasn't working so hard so that Bud could retire and downsize my life. I wanted to keep my life. Plus, I was honestly exhausted from the daily commuting. Bud was a little disconcerted over my standoffishness, but I don't think he was surprised. He knew what I wanted and why I was doing it. Quietly and without any drama, I moved from my home in Winnetka to a condo on Astor Street in 1978. Bud moved into our house in Wisconsin. That was it.

When we announced our separation, people were surprised because there had never been any histrionics or fighting between us. We actually really liked each other. Therese Benedek, whom I was still in contact with as a friend, said that Bud and I would have had an almost perfect marriage if he had ever consistently worked. We came from similar backgrounds and were good friends. He was bright. We had fun. The sex was great, and everything was fine, but it is hard when your partner doesn't earn a living or find joy in life. Certainly, there was sadness, but I had finally reached the point where I could not put up with him or go on with the show.

In the beginning I had planned to get a divorce, but Toni very practically informed me of the ramifications of that action. "You're crazy!" she said. She reminded me that if Bud and I divorced, I would lose the benefits of his air force retirement pay. I never would have thought of it, but she was right. Also, Toni, unlike her sister, Kathy, who had suggested that Bud and I split up years before, didn't want to see her parents divorced. She wanted the stability and constancy of an "us" even if we lived in separate states, even if we were dating other people.

I had gone to work because I was worried about money, and I was leaving Bud because I was sick of being the only one worrying about money. While Ira Kaufman, a stockbroker and owner of the Exchange National Bank, was then skillfully managing my assets, I couldn't afford to throw anything away. So Bud and I stayed "officially" married.

Once I was living on my own, I started "dating" Lenny Rosenfield and Bob Swartchild, a couple of elderly bachelors who were simply wonderful. Going out with them meant a good time seeing a movie and having dinner without further obligation.

In Wisconsin, Bud loved the solitude of the farm and enjoyed himself, but it was really the end of his vitality. He read, relaxed, and showed me how well he did his laundry when I came to visit. After a while, he finally decided that he wanted to get his life in order and start living again. He joined an AA group at Highland Park Hospital and even started dating for a while, but his romantic efforts were half-hearted because he still held a candle for me.

After a few months of AA meetings, Bud decided that he needed more help and went to an in-patient rehab center in New Jersey. One of the things they insisted upon was that the spouse come as well. They wanted me there for seven days. I was not pleased with the process. For one thing, I had already gone down this path with Kathy, and for another, I wasn't the one with the drinking problem—it was my estranged husband. Mostly, I felt that Bud was not really assuming much responsibility for himself or his addiction. He had checked in but wasn't willing to do the work. Still, I agreed to go for five days, not seven, as I had a hospital conference to attend.

When I got there, the staff was angry because I refused the specific order regarding the number of days in residence. I could feel their disdain for me right away. The caregivers were all recovered alcoholics, so I was seen as an outside person with a different background. The rules

I had to follow in the treatment center were meant for the patients, not the visitors. It was frustrating, and I felt confined.

The five days seemed to drag on. Bud did what he did best and withdrew. He became silent and totally dependent on the program. He liked it because he was the star patient and hero, as he was doing the "right" thing. As I heard Bud talk the new talk, I was reminded of Kathy's conscious choice to avoid all temptations because of her addictive personality, and I worried that Bud wasn't capable of making the same brave decision. He was strong, but he was also selfish and spoiled. I knew both sides of him well, and I had had all that I could take. I had basically been hung out to dry, struggling on my own while he went away to deal with his problems. I knew his alcoholism needed to be addressed, but it didn't make it any easier on me.

The exit interview made me furious. "Do you really know yourself?" the counselor asked. I felt my blood begin to boil. I came and did what they asked me to do. I followed their rules. Why was I the one being attacked? In frustration and anger, I started to cry but then dried my tears when I told them that the experience there had been one of the most unpleasant things I'd ever been through.

Although I had been defiant and unapologetic in the treatment center, I cried hot, angry tears all the way to the airport. The experience upset me so much that when a friend bumped into me at work the following week, she asked what had happened to me. I told her, and she said that how I had been treated was unforgivable and unfair. I had been made the enemy after all of my caregiving, energy, and love had been spent. I was at a low point.

In the aftermath of his stint in rehab, Bud had two years of sobriety—years he enjoyed. He lived quietly, read the AA Big Book every day, visited with his cousins, and was basically "king of the hill" in Wisconsin. He decided that there wasn't a better woman for him than me and was happy to be alone if he couldn't be with me. Sometimes he would come to the city and join me for dinner, and I'd go and see him on a weekend in the country now and then. Anybody who was an alcoholic was invited to the farm. Eventually, he did something unusual that gave him joy. He raised money to build a little house where the AA members could meet in West Bend, Wisconsin. It was a place to come together and rest and eat and support each other. "Now I know the pleasure you get from doing things for other people," he told me one day.

In the winter of 1980, Bud had another heart attack, and Toni and I went to see him in the hospital. It was odd because he didn't seem any different than usual, but on the drive back home, I confided in Toni that I thought Bud may be reaching the end, and she said she felt the same way. We had no reason for speculation; he had been through terrible things before. TB. Heart attacks. Bypasses. I had never been upset or afraid that he was going to die. But that time, I knew he was going downhill. I sensed it. Both my daughter and I did.

Bud came to Chicago one last time to have dinner with me. He asked me to come spend a week with him in Wisconsin; I think he was hoping I would move back in with him and we could restart our life together as husband and wife. I said I'd come for a visit, but I never made it because he died a few days later. It was May of 1980, and he was only sixty-three. He had been watching the farmer plow our field and died peacefully. Suddenly, my work became a bigger blessing than ever, and I got more involved with as many things as I could to cope with the sorrow, the loss, and the void.

Risk Management

Thankfully, my career at the hospital kept me busy, to say the least. Although the philosophical shift from "humanizing the hospital" to "reducing risk" was mostly nonverbal, my staff and I had long since learned what was expected of us. It was not patient comfort for its own sake but rather for the sake of the bottom line. At that time, Michael Reese had no risk management procedures, so we in the hospitality department were actually doing makeshift malpractice litigation prevention. We worked closely with Reese's legal team at the time, Max Brown and Mary Dempsey.

If a patient was dissatisfied, we were notified almost immediately and would follow up by contacting the responsible doctor. If the doctor responded with care and concern, the patient usually saw that as an "accountable" action and decided not to sue the hospital. If the doctor didn't respond, the hospital was usually in trouble.

One of the most difficult cases that I worked on concerned a child who had undergone a botched operation. The doctors refused to communicate with the family in the aftermath of what seemed to be rather egregious errors and mistakes. Later, at the University of Chicago Hospitals, the child went through a second operation to correct the one done at Reese. It was a difficult situation, and, as hard as it was to admit, I believed we were in the wrong.

The family lived in Indiana and had to be absent from work to travel back and forth during the child's recovery. They paid babysitters for their other children's care while they were in Chicago. Understandably disturbed, in a fit of anger, they told me that they were considering suing the hospital for $10 million. As a representative of the hospital, it was my job to prevent such an action. I informed the family that it would involve a long and arduous legal process before that amount of money might be awarded through litigation—and there were no guarantees. They considered what I said and came back with a request for $250,000.

As I soon discovered, though completely anguished over the circumstances, they were really nice people. Over time, we actually became so friendly that they sent my mother a get-well card when she had cataract surgery. Eventually, because our relationship had become more amicable, I felt as if I could ask them what their bottom line was. They finally disclosed what they really wanted: reimbursement for their expenses and assurance that the offending physicians would be prevented from operating in the future.

At the time, Toni was a paralegal working at a top law firm; my friend Max Brown, who had then taken a position as general counsel at Rush-Presbyterian-St. Luke's, had helped her get a job doing medical malpractice work. Toni informed me that her office had separate lawsuits against the doctors involved in our case. Knowing that other mistakes were being made as well, I took my courage in my hands and went to Dr. Sidney Lee, Reese's president at the time. I asked Dr. Lee whether he thought the situation merited a review of the doctors, and he confirmed that it did. He suggested that I talk to the head of surgery to perform the review.

To accuse doctors of doing something wrong was scary. I walked a thin line between representing the hospital's medical staff and protecting the patients. In reality, I probably could have been thrown out, but I wasn't. In fact, Reese agreed to an independent review panel composed of ten doctors who would evaluate the case. I presented the information as I knew it and waited for their response. I let the panel know that all the hospital needed to settle was $6,918, to take care of the family's expenses, but reiterated that the family insisted that the doctors be fired.

In the end, the review found at least ten instances where these pediatric surgeons had made mistakes. The panel voted them guilty, and they were dismissed. The doctors' response was, unbelievably, quite unapologetic. At first, they seemed to ignore the judgment, and then they fought it. They didn't want their public records to be harmed, so when it looked as if they would be fired, they left on their own accord and somehow managed to keep clean records. In fact, they were able to secure new positions at Rush-Presbyterian-St. Luke's, but I called Max to alert him that trouble was headed his way.

When I think about what I accomplished for Michael Reese in terms of negotiating a fair settlement and forcing out bad doctors, it seems bizarre that the value of our role as patient representatives wasn't acknowledged to a greater degree. We were doing real, measureable work to save the hospital money, time, and resources. I didn't complain, however, because I never got over feeling grateful that I had the job in the first place and was able to make such a difference in the lives of so many people.

Daughter Drama

The sticky situation at the hospital and Bud's recent death weren't the only dramatic events at the time. I soon learned that after twelve years of marriage, Kathy would be getting divorced. Steve had not been a good husband to her, and she had turned to drinking to ease the unhappiness. Although she had enjoyed "wifing," as she called it, and made a lot of friends in California, she had lost herself somehow. In 1981, she was sad, broke, miserable, and, worst of all, as I feared, an alcoholic.

The day she got divorced, she was able to stop drinking, but she had used up all of her funds by then and needed more support than AA could give her. She reached out and asked Toni whether she could live with her. Now acting more like the older sister than the younger one, Toni of course said yes.

I think in the beginning Toni was happy to have her sister living with her. After a period of being alone, she seemed to enjoy the companionship. Toni had had a couple of serious relationships, but they were complicated and unsatisfying, and nothing ever stuck. She had almost been engaged once and then carried on a lengthy affair with a married man. By the time Kathy moved in with Toni, she, too, was tired of men. At first, the girls enjoyed each other's company, and Kathy was grateful to Toni for her support. But eventually, Toni got sick of her sister doing nothing. Toni was busy, as usual, but Kathy didn't seem to have any interests and seldom left the house.

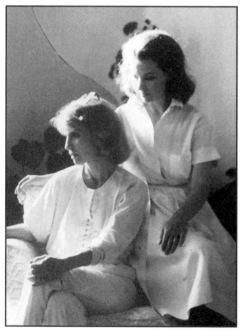

Kathy moved in with Toni after each had trouble with the men in their lives. The sisters relied on each other for support but sometimes experienced tension in their relationship.

Eventually, Toni told Kathy that she had to get a job or move out. Toni said that it was one of the most difficult things she ever did, and I could certainly empathize, having undergone a similar situation with their father. Toni's ultimatum was just the nudge Kathy needed. She got a job, first in a flower shop and then at Plunkett Furniture, an established family-owned furniture store with several locations in Chicago. It was a job she really enjoyed. She was responsible for the appearance of the store and maintenance of inventory. As usual, she excelled in her position and was highly regarded by all the Plunketts. When they opened a store in St. Louis, she was asked to manage it. That opportunity gave her back her drive.

Toni, however, took a different path. In 1986, when she turned forty, she decided to give herself the life she had always wanted to share with a family of her own, even if she had to do it alone. She bought a beautiful house in Winnetka and for all practical purposes dropped out of her own life. Usually social and outgoing, she spent all her time at home and didn't go out with any of her friends. I was concerned, but if I knew anything about her, it was that she could take care of herself and would be fine on her own, if that's what she thought would make her happy.

Bill Kirby

After Bud's death, beyond my professional life I also had a romantic one. About a year after Bud died, my good friend and one of Chicago's best-loved philanthropists Bootsie Nathan and her husband, Joe, introduced me to their lawyer, Bill Kirby, over dinner at the Drake Hotel. William T. Kirby had been John MacArthur's lawyer for more than twenty-five years. Although the legendary billionaire had spent his life amassing great wealth, he had no real interest in philanthropy when he was alive. But instead of leaving his money to his estranged children, his directive to Bill was simple: "When I die, I want you to establish a foundation in my name."

With an initial portfolio of $800 million, Bill established and helmed the John D. and Catherine T. MacArthur Foundation, creating one of the most dynamic organizations of its kind. Through shrewd investments and management, Bill transformed the endowment into a portfolio worth more than $3 billion in assets while fulfilling its mission to support individuals and organizations working in the areas of peace, conservation, health, and education.

Bill called me right away after we met, and we dated for a number of years and became good friends. I wasn't really up for a romance at the time but loved his company. He was also dating other women then, but we regularly went dancing and to the theater. He was always inviting me to events with his kids, whom I got to know as well.

Bill Kirby, who established the John D. and Catherine T. MacArthur Foundation, was a wonderful friend and a marvelous person—and also once a romantic interest.

In 1990, Toni convinced me that I should lighten my load of responsibilities by selling the farm in Wisconsin. It had been rented, and I turned to Bill for help in moving out the current tenant. So on a sunny October day, I picked Bill up at the Drake Towers, where he had an apartment. He looked so dashing and was in such good spirits. I'll never forget his outfit. He always dressed well, but on that particular day he looked like an English lord dressed for a foxhunt, perfect for the Wisconsin wilderness.

The two-hour drive was pleasant. After we arrived and dropped off our things at the family house, we walked up the hill to the little farmhouse. When we got there, we discovered that the tenant was gone but a large mess remained. Piles of garbage littered every room—three thousand pounds' worth to be exact—but I tried not to overreact. The important thing was that the renter was gone and we had avoided what could have been a nasty altercation.

I showed Bill the beautiful old barn where Bud's cattle had once been, and we enjoyed the view of the entire expanse of the lake. We walked through lilac bushes and groves of apple trees to the shore, taking in the sunshine and autumn leaves, and then we went back down the hill for lunch.

Bill seated himself at the table that faced the lake and began to talk as I set out the lunch I had brought for us. He was a great raconteur. Eventually, I sat down next to him, looking out at the view, listening to him chatting happily. Suddenly, he stopped talking. I looked at him and realized instantly that he was not searching for a word; he had stopped living! Just like that, he had passed away in front of me. I was so panicked that I got up and started screaming, "You can't do this!" in dire hope I could revive him.

With my heart racing, I started making calls. First, I tried to call Toni, but I was in such a panic that I could not remember her phone number—and I am known for my keen memory and recall of numbers, so this was highly unusual. I ended up calling the village, where I had friends, the Bergmans, who owned a store, and asked them to send an ambulance right away, even though I knew that Bill was already dead. The scene was tragic and became only more unbelievable as onlookers arrived at the farm. The real estate agent who was scheduled to list the house for sale arrived for his appointment. The coroner arrived, as well as representatives from the funeral home in West Bend. I was overwhelmed by my own shock and the commotion going on all around me.

Several days later, back in Chicago, the mass for Bill was conducted at Holy Name Cathedral. At the funeral, his son told me he was glad that his father was with me when he died. In his obituary in *The New York Times*, Bill was said to have passed away while visiting friends in Wisconsin. He truly was a dear friend, and the act of witnessing his death was extremely disconcerting.

Afterward, I arranged to follow through on the sale of the farm. I was ready to be rid of a place with so many unhappy memories. I sold the house and the three acres surrounding it to a young family; the rest of the land went to a neighboring farmer. In one fell swoop I had lost my friend and closed another chapter of my life—a life that seemed very empty to me at the time.

I.O.U.

Once again, I turned to my career to fill the void. At Michael Reese, the last president I worked for asked me to teach four thousand employees how to improve their service performance. In those days hospitals were just beginning to become more competitive. Treating patients as customers was part of the market orientation. The job really should have been given to the head of human resources because it involved organizational development and training, but I responded positively to the request to teach by drawing on my own educational background and by hiring one of the best hospital consultants in the country. Kristi Peterson did research on all of the positions in the hospital, wrote the training curriculum, and developed the implementation plan. We selected about twenty of our customer service "stars" to help us roll out the program.

The hospital's slogan at the time was "Michael Reese—making it better for everybody," a concept I fully supported. I felt as if I was always trying to make Reese better for everyone: patients, doctors, nurses, and employees alike. They were all important to the hospital's success. I suggested that we call our program the I.O.U. Program. The concept cascaded from a global mission to a personal one: everybody in the hospital owed every patient the best care possible, just as every leader owed the employees the best possible work experience. And I, personally, owed the hospital and the employees a super outcome.

To kick off the program, we held an "I.O.U. fest," where the top brass of the hospital stepped in to provide service in the cafeteria. The experience humanized them considerably. After that, classes were scheduled around the clock from November to January for all four thousand employees, many of whom met each other for the first time in those classes.

I worked to create an atmosphere where all employees, including both the low-paid and high-paid workers, were acknowledged for their hard work and commitment. By giving awards for special service and performance to those who deserved them and by implementing programs such as employee of the week, month, or quarter, I helped to change the internal culture in the hospital. Some of the results were quite dramatic.

One of my favorite examples came from a woman who was in charge of registering people for same-day surgeries. She was very smart and effective at her job, but she was a bit of a sourpuss. One day, she remarked that nobody ever smiled at her. I suggested she try it herself.

"Try what?" she asked, flabbergasted.

"Smiling," I said, with a genuine smile on my face. "*You* never smile at anyone."

Though it couldn't have been easy at first, she tried it. She looked stiff, but she kept at it. As people reciprocated with grins of their own, she smiled more. By the time she was voted employee of the year, her smiles had become second nature. Looking back, I think she just didn't realize the power of a friendly face.

From a patient care standpoint, I'll never forget a young man we cared for who was a student at the University of Chicago. He had been beaten during a robbery and was in a coma. His chances for recovery or rehabilitation were grim. Even the doctor was doubtful. However, I had heard that talking to a person in a coma helped with the recovery. So, every day, I went into his room and held his hand and talked to him. His only relatives in Chicago were an aunt and uncle, and I encouraged them to spend as much time with him as they could. The nurses all talked to him as well. One day when I walked in, he opened his eyes. He went on to recover, successfully complete rehab, and finish his degree. He even came back to Michael Reese and asked for a job with us. Unfortunately, we didn't have any openings at the time, but if we had, I know he would have been hired on the spot. He was the perfect testimony to the patient-centered care I dedicated myself to developing for those served by Reese in the city of Chicago and in the medical community at large.

Dr. Eddie Newman

In addition to I.O.U. training, I still had all of the rest of my duties to perform, which included visiting patients, solving problems, being a notary public, managing staff, and anticipating wants before they became needs. Above all, my job was to make it easy for people to sail through the system and to make sure they were happy with the hospital. Within fifteen minutes of a patient's admission, one of my staff members was in his or her room to give information and let the patient know that we were available for whatever might be needed.

Everyone admitted to the hospital was important, but we tended to take extra-special care of Dr. Eddie Newman's flock of famous, wealthy, or celebrity patients. Edward Newman was a brilliant internist, nationally renowned for being the best diagnostician at Michael Reese. He had an irreverent foul mouth that he (and most people, really) delighted in and was also one of the most caring and kind individuals I have ever known. I grew up with him in Hyde Park, so I knew what to expect from him.

Still, Newman was not to be underestimated. On my second day, he came into my office with a movable holder for IV drips and told me to tell the president to have them cleaned. I was shocked! He found fault with things all the time—but, I have to admit, not usually inappropriately. Correcting the faults—of which he continually made me aware—took a lot of man-hours and eventually occupied a large portion of my time and energy.

But long before I knew him in a professional context, I knew Dr. Newman was "the" doctor to see, and, naturally, the wealthy and famous sought him out. I saw quite a few stars of the day pass in and out of Reese, even comforting some of them when they were scared. But, you know what they say about doctor-patient confidentiality! My lips are sealed.

In addition to Dr. Newman and his patients, there was an entire hospital full of patients and doctors to tend to and never a dull moment. I found myself comforting a drug addict who threw a telephone at my head, caring for a pregnant lawyer arguing a case from the delivery room, and dealing with a patient who found a cockroach in her Coke.

I had a particularly memorable meeting with Jay and Bob Pritzker when they were in the hospital visiting their father, A. N. Pritzker. The sons came every morning to see their father, and we became very friendly and would meet for coffee. I knew the Pritzkers socially and was well aware that Ray Drymalski, the president of the Lincoln Park Zoo Board, had long been after Bob for a contribution to the zoo. His initial gift to the zoo had been $15,000, but I knew he would do more if only I could cast the zoo's needs in a way that would resonate with his and his family's interests.

Once I had my strategy clear in my head, I opened up the conversation by asking him very nicely—but bluntly—"What are you *really* going do about the zoo?"

He stood up, put his arms around me, and said, "Marion, I love ya! How's a million dollars?" I almost dropped dead. That million dollars went toward the creation of the Pritzker Children's Zoo.

Eventually, at age seventy, after having been part of so many groundbreaking aspects of Michael Reese Hospital, I decided it was time to move on. I felt as if I had effected positive changes in patient-centered care and medical research. It was a good professional run, and I was proud of my accomplishments, building a successful department from nothing and creating real change in the medical institution.

As a final favor to John Gunn, a friend and colleague from Reese, I took a trip to New York City with him to help him get settled in his new position at Sloan-Kettering. He had initially turned down the request from the Rockefellers to work there, but when Lawrence Rockefeller himself met John at the plane on his third visit there, John finally said yes. I introduced him to all my friends and contacts in the city, and we took in the sights, even seeing a David Mamet play, *Edmond*, produced by my cousin David Weil. They held the curtain for us because we were running late. It was quite an experience! To this day, John retains his position at Sloan-Kettering and does a magnificent job.

Opportunities Arise

With my career at Reese coming to an end and with Bud, as well as Bill Kirby, gone, my loneliness sometimes got the best of me. I found the most difficult thing about being a single woman was not having an escort when I needed one. I had developed a warm friendship with Ed Hurd and even met his children when they visited. He took me to some big parties, and we had a lot of fun together. My bachelor friends Lenny and Bob were fine, but they had their own lives and circle of friends. Lenny introduced me to his widowed brother, Marty.

The first time Marty took me out, we went to a Printer's Row restaurant. He didn't want anybody to see me with him, lest it get out that he was dating. The second time, we went to the International Club at the Drake Hotel, and Lenny came along as chaperone to guard Marty's reputation as an unattached bachelor. Eventually, Marty agreed to let it be known publicly that we were dating, but it was a very colorless experience, and I was happy to move on.

I then started going out with Dr. Irving (Bud) Stein. His deceased wife was a close friend of mine, and I had known them both for years. I enjoyed his company, and everybody wanted us to get married, but there was no spark, and eventually we just drifted apart.

Next was Jeffrey Fried, whom I dated happily for a year. We traveled together to Austria and Arizona. Then he sold his business and did something I didn't want to do—he retired to Florida. He loved music and was very generous. I had flowers every week. He really had hoped we could marry, but I had no desire to waste away the rest of my life sipping piña coladas and playing shuffleboard in Boca Raton.

Enter Ted Gross, at the time the recently appointed president of Roosevelt University. He had moved to Chicago in 1988 from New York, where he had been the dean of the College of Letters and Science at the State University of New York at Purchase. When I met Ted through Alan Anixter in early 1991, I still had several other suitors but knew I was not interested in any of them for a permanent relationship. I was also between projects, in terms of employment.

When I met Ted Gross, he had recently become the president of Roosevelt University. I began exploring new opportunities to expand my fund-raising and bring in more money for student scholarships at Roosevelt, and during that time, Ted and I grew close.

I worked briefly for a company called Heartlink and in addition was serving on the boards of the Chicago International Film Festival, the Community Review Standards Panel, and the Small Grants Foundation for the Chicago Foundation for Education. I was also an active member of the Women's Association of the Chicago Symphony and retained my position on the Lincoln Park Zoo Board, but I was looking for another professional challenge.

Anixter, owner of one of the leading communication products distribution companies in the world, was on Roosevelt's board of directors. He arranged for me to meet Ted because he wanted me to help the urban university raise money for scholarships. I knew nothing about Roosevelt or Ted, but I felt the prospect had appeal and agreed to a meeting. I asked my friend Bootsie Nathan to come with me to help evaluate Ted, as well as the employment opportunity.

We all met at the swanky Pump Room in the Ambassador East Hotel. It was extremely pleasant. Dr. Gross was a rather meat-and-potatoes kind of academic who was completely comfortable in his world of ideas. Coming from New York, he had a limited number of contacts in Chicago and was very up front about his needs for fund-raising, his passion for the school, and his belief in the students. He was also exceptionally charming. After the meeting, Bootsie gave me a thumbs-up and suggested I go to work for Roosevelt University.

Although I had been fund-raising for years, when I started working for Roosevelt, one of the first things I did was go to Gonser Gerber Tinker Stuhr, professional advisors on fund-raising. After a review of my plans, they told me that the system I was using was similar to the one they recommended to their clients. The staff and I became friends, and we spoke at each other's meetings. It felt good knowing I was on the right track—and always had been.

I agreed to raise money for scholarships at Roosevelt and in the process began to get to know a little bit about Ted. His wife was dying at the time, and he was shrouded in sadness yet compelled to perform as an energetic and enthusiastic leader. One of the things Ted asked me to do was create a multiethnic board, reflecting the school's diversity, that would raise money for performing arts scholarships in Roosevelt's Music Conservatory. I was so impressed with the student musicians from around the world that I did so eagerly.

In addition, I decided that the Auditorium Building, which housed the music school, should be restored to as much of its previous glory as possible. Built by Louis Sullivan and Dankmar Adler, it had been one of the first buildings to be lit by electric light. When it opened in 1889, it boasted a four-thousand-seat auditorium, a hotel, and an office tower. The building had fallen into disuse after the Depression, ending up as a place for rock concerts, at which no one noticed the peeling paint or rickety seats. In 1946, the building became part of Roosevelt University. Its renovation and revitalization became one of my many projects, and I was skillfully advised by the brilliant Chicago architect Larry Booth.

Not long after I started at Roosevelt, Ted's wife died. He was obviously lost without her. We spent increasing amounts of time together because my job was to introduce him to influential people in Chicago business and society. Actually, the excitement we both felt as we met with people and explained the university's mission and Ted's vision was a catalyst in the development of our relationship. We began dating that summer. He was good company, but our passion for the university compensated for the lack of passion between us.

In November of 1991 I went to Russia with a friend, Eve Eiseman, and had a fabulous time. I came back in January after the holidays, and Ted and I got more serious and decided to get married. The marriage was more for public consumption than out of our own particular desire or need. He was president of a university, and if we wanted to live together, he thought we should be married. Out of respect for his wife, I insisted that we wait until she had been deceased for a year before we tied the knot. He was ready for things to move faster but agreed to my request.

Ted announced our engagement and upcoming marriage publicly at a party held at Chicago's upscale private club the Casino. As it turned out, not everyone liked the idea of our proposed union. Toni didn't like Ted from the start and was furious. Joining in the chorus of lament was a visibly pained Alan Tishman. I had dinner with Tish at Coco Pazzo immediately before I announced my engagement to Ted.

"How can you do that to me?" he asked after I told him. He was clearly upset. I told him that he was crazy and reminded him that he was married.

"Yes," he admitted, "but I don't want you to go through with this."

His reaction was odd because he didn't even know Ted at the time. It was, however, the beginning of the end of our deep lifelong friendship, as Tish developed Alzheimer's disease not long after we met that final time for dinner.

More important than wedding plans was the decision about where we would live. Ted was living in an apartment at One Magnificent Mile. He loved it, but the apartment was cramped, and his wife had passed away in their bedroom. My apartment on Astor Street was cheery but too small for the two of us.

However, in my building, just a few floors up, I discovered a much larger apartment for sale. It was the perfect size for entertaining, which would be important for my fund-raising efforts for the university. Before we could make any decisions about what to do about the real estate investment, we had to leave the country in an attempt to raise money for Roosevelt.

We had accepted an invitation from a Roosevelt alumnus to go to Korea. The man was a politician, and he had promised a gift for the school. But by the time we got there, he had just lost his bid for office, so the school didn't get a cent. Nonetheless, he and his wife were extremely hospitable, and we enjoyed our visit in Seoul.

From Korea, I continued long-distance negotiations on the apartment in my building. We secured a mortgage for the new place, and we both sold our former residences. By the time we returned from Korea, everything was well under way with our transition, both residentially and matrimonially.

I married Ted Gross on May 24, 1992, at Lake Shore Country Club. Nearly three hundred people were in attendance, but I can't say we had a lot of well-wishers. Kathy was enthusiastic but said she just wanted me to be happy. Toni, however, was extremely upset and felt that we had moved too quickly. Ted's kids were not all that pleased, either. My mother was one of the only people who supported us. As a 102-½-year-old mother of the bride, she came to the ceremony and shared in the celebration. Her support meant the world to me.

The day after the wedding, Ted and I left for Santa Fe, New Mexico, for a short three-day honeymoon so we would be back in time for Roosevelt's graduation ceremonies. Later in the summer we went to the island of Crete in Greece for a longer honeymoon getaway.

I quickly learned that in many ways Ted was a good companion. Unlike Bud, he didn't drink, and I appreciated that. Also, he was very bright and could easily quote from literature. He loved the theater, music, the arts, and travel. We were culturally in tune, but it was almost as if he knew that he was emotionally cold and whatever he lacked in terms of warmth, he attempted to compensate with a show of good will whenever possible.

Ted Gross and I married and built our life around our dedication to a shared passion, supporting Roosevelt University.

When our new apartment was ready later that summer, I simply moved all of my things up a few floors—furniture, window treatments, everything. This home set the stage for performances we would host on behalf of the university. In our living room we held concerts to promote the students and showcase the school. It was almost as if those kids were our own. After all, they were what we had in common. Ted and I worked hard together for the university, a cause we both truly believed in and cared about.

I was even honored for my achievements at Roosevelt and elsewhere, with an award from Little City and Sidney Port. Also being honored was my good friend Desirée Rogers, who at the time headed the Illinois Lottery. I was flattered to be recognized for my work throughout the city and couldn't wait to continue making things better at Roosevelt.

Benefiting Roosevelt

I assembled the Chicago Board at Roosevelt University, with assistance from Ted, to raise funds for scholarships and awareness of the musical college. It was such an exciting time. The school was flowering, and I was able to pack the board with a selection of Chicago's movers and shakers as diverse as the population of the school.

I was invited by Peter Kovler on a trip to Washington, D.C., to celebrate the dedication of the Roosevelt memorial, including this statue of Eleanor.

Alicia Valentine-Goldfarb, a well-known socialite, had introduced me to John Lynch from LaSalle Bank, and he gave me $30,000 to get us going. I asked a number of esteemed men from the Lincoln Park Zoo Board (Hossein Youssefi, Howard Morgan, and Ron Culp), and they all joined us. I invited Marsha Goldstein, who was a graduate of Roosevelt and owner of a Chicago destination management services company called My Kind of Town, to join us, along with Kathleen Drennan, whom I had met at Heartlink, and Kristi Peterson, the consultant who designed our I.O.U. Program at Michael Reese. Ted introduced me to real estate developer and author Dempsey Travis; Ping Tom, who was head of the Chinatown revitalization project; and Arthur Morimitsu, president of the Japanese American Service Committee and a leader of the campaign for monetary compensation for Japanese Americans forced into internment camps during WWII. Stan Lewin, co-owner of a hot and ascending advertising and marketing firm, came on board, as did Hyde Park Bank President Tim Goodsell; public relations maven Judi Schindler; commercial real estate investment manager Keith Pochter; friends Josie Strauss, Jane Davis, and Anne Davis; and banker Gwen Cohen of Morgan Stanley. In addition, Terry Spencer Hesser wrote and produced some lovely videos to promote the school, one of which was a one-hour history of the beautiful and historic Auditorium Building that aired on PBS and snagged two Emmy nominations.

After the creation of our board, I started looking for funding by going to people I knew who had an interest in Roosevelt, including alumni, music lovers, and architecture buffs. Seymour Persky, a graduate, had all three credentials and gave us money to redo the front of the Auditorium Building and replace the original lighting in the lobby. He was also heavily involved in restoring the Sullivan Room, where he replaced the fireplace with a model more fitting of the original design of the room. We brought the room to life again. Both Ann Lurie and Abby McCormick O'Neil generously hosted lovely and lavish musical evenings at their homes in support of Roosevelt.

Another project, and a much bigger one, was the restoration of Ganz Hall, the small concert hall created by the famous pianist Rudolph Ganz. We rehabbed the space by cleaning the paintings and installing new carpets. Under my leadership and direction, the board brought in replicas of the original lightoliers designed by Louis Sullivan.

These important rooms had been neglected, and we brought them back
to their full glory so they could be enjoyed by all.

*Ted and I greatly enjoyed celebrating my fund-raising success during my many star-
studded benefits for Roosevelt.*

For my own debut benefit event for Roosevelt, I wanted the
entertainment to be high-quality jazz. To get the money to bring in
such talent, board member Ron Culp took me to meet Robert Lauer,
head of development for Sara Lee and a lover of jazz music. Mr. Lauer
gave me $85,000, and our first benefit, a jazz concert to be held in the
partially restored and acoustically perfect Auditorium Theater, was
arranged.

Planning was well under way when, one morning, I dashed to
answer the telephone at home and slipped on a newly polished floor.
I broke my wrist but somehow managed to drive myself to the emergency room at Northwestern Memorial Hospital. I called my old friend
Dr. Eddie Newman, and he arranged for a hand specialist to do the surgery and apply the cast. As I convalesced, I wrote out the seating chart
for the benefit with my left hand.

For my second Roosevelt benefit, I worked closely with Earl Schub, head of Roosevelt's music department at the time, and we decided to do a concert at Symphony Hall featuring internationally famous opera singer Kiri Te Kanawa.

We then secured Itzhak Perlman to perform a concert at Symphony Hall, followed by a dinner at the Chicago Club. The scale of the benefit had increased immensely. We took over both the ballroom and the grill. Entertaining Mr. Perlman was the best part of the planning. The day of the benefit, I had a lot to do, but when he called at noon and asked what our lunch plans were, I couldn't turn him down. He suggested Woo Lae Oak, a new restaurant, and I immediately called Ted and told him to meet us there. I ordered a limo and called event cochairs Josie Strauss and Jane Davis to keep him busy. Within an hour, we were seated in a private room at the restaurant, where Itzhak ordered food for all of us and entertained us for two and a half hours. He was full of stories; all were funny and delightful. We had a ball. By the time we left lunch, I had to go home, change, and hurry back for the benefit.

One of my fondest memories of my benefits for Roosevelt University was meeting and spending time with violinist Itzhak Perlman.

When I got to the event, everyone was frantic. A staff person with gorgeous calligraphy was supposed to do our tickets but had decided to walk out that morning without finishing because she wasn't feeling well. I almost went bonkers. Josie stood at the top of the stairs and said, as everybody was going a little cuckoo, "I don't get involved in things like this." Fortunately, I had brought my guest list, so as people walked up the stairs, the greeters could check them off. The show went on, and all in all, it was a hugely successful concert, but, to me, the most fun was visiting with Itzhak.

Marilyn Horne performing at the Auditorium Theater was next. The night before her concert, she was desperately ill. I was concerned for her health but also for our schedule! As I waited for the final word on whether she would perform, I wondered to myself what, exactly, I was supposed to do if she couldn't make it. But at 5 p.m., they finally agreed that she would be able to take the stage. What a trouper! She did the whole show with a fever and even stayed for the after-party.

Eventually, the board decided that having all of the events "cabaret style" at the Hilton Hotel, where we could use multiple rooms for different functions, was easier than running from one place to another after the performance. The Hilton and, in particular, the catering manager, Mr. Chen, were both marvelous. I would sell forty-two tables at $5,000 each and pack the room before the invitations were even mailed.

Recognition and Recovery

The Roosevelt benefits had found a new home and continued to be successful and a lot of fun—so much so that in the spring of 1997, the premiere issue of *The American Benefactor* featured an article about me and several other nationally celebrated fund-raisers, entitled "America's

Greatest Rainmakers: They Work Hard, Do Good, Raise Millions, and Manage to Make It All Look Like a Party." I was extremely flattered!

In an article in The American Benefactor *magazine featuring five women fund-raisers, I was the only one who was not independently wealthy. I am proud of my accomplishments and flattered to have been profiled.*

At the time I was very busy, holding bigger and bigger benefit events for Roosevelt. We had Frank Sinatra Jr. perform, and socialite Donna LaPietra arranged for a beautiful Italian-themed dinner. The décor was perfect: long tables covered with red and white checked tablecloths and bottles of wine, as well as special cookies for everyone. Sadly, it was not terribly successful in terms of ticket sales because people didn't really know who Frank was at the time, but in the end the audience gave him a standing ovation. His performance was marvelous, and no one was more thrilled than he was. I don't think anybody had ever paid as much attention to him as we did. All during the planning, he would telephone me every night at 10 p.m. and with a booming voice say, "Marion, this is Frank."

For Harry Belafonte, the board decided on an island theme, but signals got crossed, and the florists from Ronsley didn't arrive until 5 p.m. to start setting up the centerpieces of tropical orchids and bamboo. Mr. Belafonte had just gotten off a plane from London and wanted to rehearse in private before the show. By 5:30, the cocktail reception had started outside the ballroom. Finally, just before the show was scheduled to start at 7:00, a dozen people ran in to prepare the ballroom, and it all came together. Of course, it was a lovely evening, but in the meantime I was going crazy!

We had several successful benefits with other stars, including Tony Bennett, Rosemary Clooney, Michael Feinstein, and Nancy Wilson, but probably my most memorable experience of all was with Bill Cosby. He had agreed to perform for the university free of charge if I could raise more money for Roosevelt than I ever had before. I shot for the moon and named my price at $1 million. He wanted to support the university for his friend Ramsey Lewis, internationally renowned jazz pianist, also a close friend of mine. Bill was so wonderful and performed before a packed house. It was a fantastically fun (and funny) time! However, what wasn't fun was having to be taken to the benefit in a wheelchair. Kathy had come from St. Louis to take me.

My benefits for Roosevelt continued to be successful and included stars such as Harry Belafonte, Tony Bennett, Nancy Wilson, and—my favorite and the most successful of all—Bill Cosby.

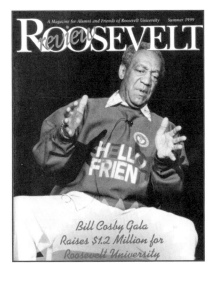

During the hectic pace of planning, I began to realize that Ted and I were not getting enough exercise. I hadn't played tennis in years, but I thought it might be fun for us to play together. We joined Midtown Tennis Club but ended up playing separately. Early on in our lessons, I realized that Ted played only to win, too intense for me. In an amazing contrast to his mild social demeanor, on the court he revealed his other side. He was out to kill, and I just wanted to have a nice time. So I let Ted's instructor go to war with Ted's repressed inner self, and I joined a class.

I was eighty years old at the time but managed to somehow keep up with the class, until one day when we had to do a crazy exercise of running around the court while hitting the ball backhanded. I tripped and crashed to the ground. Within seconds I was hemorrhaging and couldn't move. Ted was called.

"What are you doing on the floor?" he asked me.

"Sorry," I said. "I fell down."

In severe pain, I was taken to the nearest hospital, Illinois Masonic, in an ambulance. Lying on that gurney, I realized that I had to act on my own behalf—as my own patient representative. From the hospital's emergency room, I called Eddie Newman. He told me in no uncertain terms to "get my ass over to Northwestern," where he would have Dr. Richard Wixson waiting for me. I called Toni, and she met us at Northwestern Memorial Hospital, where they discovered that my bones were shattered in pieces from my hip to my knee.

As the nurses administered morphine for the pain, Dr. Wixson informed Toni and Ted that he would do his best to treat me but he wasn't sure I would ever walk again. He said he'd never seen such a bad break. Ironically, at Northwestern Memorial Hospital—one of the best hospitals in the country—they did what I had so painstakingly trained the Michael Reese employees not to do: they left me on a gurney and walked away. I had to smile at the irony.

The next day, Dr. Wixson put me back together with plates and screws because my bones were broken in so many places. Later, he told me that he was afraid I would have a limp. I said, determined, "No, I won't limp." I did what I could in terms of rehab, but walking was very difficult. I was always afraid I would collapse or loosen my plates. I put lifts in my shoes and tried my best to resume my life. For one thing, I had the Bill Cosby event—and the show absolutely had to go on! I ended up beating my million-dollar goal by raising $1.2 million. Always a fan of visualization, I believed (and still do) that if you dream it, you can do it.

After spending months raising money from my bed, I was awarded a plaque from the members of the board I had assembled. It read:

To Marion:

You define grace and dignity. Your vision and leadership are matched by your unending enthusiasm and limitless energy. You inspire us all.

With love and admiration,

The Chicago Board of Roosevelt University

Around this time I also received other accolades. In April of 2000, *Chicago* magazine featured two photos of me beneath the caption "The Arm Twister." Marcia Froelke Coburn wrote, "Sweet, soft-spoken Marion Simon, a local force in philanthropic fund-raising, has refined the art of persuading people to part with large sums of money."

Friends

My life has been so much fun and has been made even more so by all the wonderful people who have filled it with memories I will always cherish.

Jerry and Josie Strauss have been my friends forever and ever and ever. Jerry was a friend of Bud's at Brown University, and Josie was a childhood friend. We've been there for each other in good times and in bad.

Marsha Goldstein (far left) is a remarkable woman who owns the successful tour business My Kind of Town and helped with Roosevelt benefits over the years. Donna LaPietra (far right) served on the committee for the Roosevelt benefit featuring Frank Sinatra Jr.

The women of the Crystal Ball: Eve Eiseman (left) and Jane Davis (center) carried the torch in planning many wonderful events to come for the Medical Research Institute Council at Michael Reese Hospital.

Mary O'Leary (right) is a dear friend I met when working at Reese. She was in nursing, and we became very close in both our personal and professional lives. Margo Adams (left) was the daughter of my best friend Betty Hirsch (Schultz), and she considers herself another daughter of mine. We've been very attached since her mother died.

Anna Tomaschewski was simply a lovely lady. She lived with me for five years and helped while Toni was ill and stayed on to assist me in my day-to-day life. Her companionship and caring meant the world to me. She died in 2012, and I will miss her dearly.

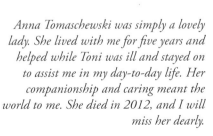

Sisters Sally Salzer (left) and Barbara Svarz (right) are Bud's cousins from Milwaukee. Their mother, Bud's cousin Dolores Mann, was one of my closest friends in the Simon family. These two wonderful women are tasked with taking care of me, and they do an exceptional job!

Two of my best and oldest friends from my childhood! I have known Jane Birkenstein (left) since nursery school and Marjorie Sachs (center) basically since I was born!

I attended a later incarnation of the Crystal Ball with my friend Ed Hurd after Bud had passed away. Everyone wanted to know who my escort was, and he said, "Let everybody worry who the silver fox is you're with."

Ramsey Lewis, the Grammy Award–winning jazz pianist, is my dear friend. He was the one responsible for helping me bring in Bill Cosby for my most successful benefit for Roosevelt University.

Family members can be friends, too! Here Bud and I (far left) are shown with his sister Libby and her husband, George Sturm, and his brother Bill and his wife, Joanie Simon. As an only child, I was so excited to have sisters and brothers of my own, even if they were in-laws.

Abby McCormick O'Neil and her husband, Carroll Joynes, and Joan and Robert Feitler are good friends. O'Neil is the chairman of the Board of Trustees of Harris Theatre, and Robert Feitler is chairman of the Board of Governors of the Smart Museum of Art.

For my ninetieth birthday, my friends and neighbors Don Raney and Jaymes Richardson ("the boys") had a doll made in my exact image! Celebrating at the party were Betsey and Dale Pinkert and Barbara Bluhm-Kaul and Don Kaul. The Pinkerts were friends in medical research and part of the Alliance Française; Betsey was also involved with the Crystal Ball and helped to plan the fiftieth-anniversary celebration for MRIC.

At a spry and sophisticated ninety-six, my first cousin Eleanor Elisberg Miller is shown with her daughter, Janice Goldman, celebrating my ninetieth birthday.

Kristi Peterson is a longtime friend and colleague, whom I brought in to help develop the successful I.O.U. Program at Reese.

Bill Kurtis is my dear, dear friend. In the special memento guestbook for my ninetieth birthday, he wrote, "I love you!"

Abra Prentice Wilkin, board member of the Lincoln Park Zoo, is a special friend. We have lunch every summer. Here she is shown giving a memorable speech at my ninetieth birthday.

My extended family members in the Simon clan are shown at a reunion at their "compound" at Cedar Lake, Wisconsin. The many generations have meant so much to me.

Dogs

I've been fortunate enough to have some wonderful canine companions. My life wouldn't have been the same without them!

Sandy was one of our first dogs, and Kathy was particularly fond of him. If I remember correctly, the shade of red in her hair was close to that in his mane!

Kathy was also close with Tippy, our beagle.

Duchess was a special friend. I called her my "city dog."

Josie and her daughter, Demitasse, were gorgeous poodles (a mini and a toy).

Lucy was given to me by my close friends and neighbors Don Raney and Jaymes Richardson.

Travel

Traveling has been one of my great passions in life. Some of my most memorable trips were to Fiji and Bora Bora, Russia, and China.

 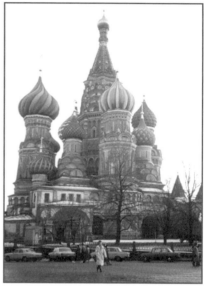

PART V

Mourning My Mother

As great as everything was going for me professionally, personally, things were complicated and becoming more so. I've never run away from things and always faced what had to be. So when my mother told me that she had read an article in a Florida newspaper about the "hemlock formula" for an easy death, I knew that she was finished with her life.

My mother lived well into her hundreds. On her one-hundredth birthday, her granddaughters and I gave her a sentimental gift of a red chair, symbolic of one she sat in when she was a little girl in school. When she reached age 106, she received a note from President Bill Clinton.

THE WHITE HOUSE
WASHINGTON

June 14, 1995

Mrs. Lillian Ellisberg
Apartment 11C
3150 North Lake Shore
Chicago, Illinois 60657

Dear Mrs. Ellisberg:

    Happy 106th Birthday! Hillary and I
wish you a memorable celebration, and we
hope that the coming year brings you great
happiness and good health.

Sincerely,

Bill Clinton

She was 106 years old and still living independently in an apartment of her own. Although she had lived a quiet life, she had retained lifelong friends and traveled in her nineties to Ocho Rios, Jamaica, as well as Mexico and Palm Beach. In addition, she volunteered at Saint Joseph Hospital. When she applied, she was in her eighties but told them she was only seventy. She worked there through her ninety-seventh birthday, loving it and doing a very good job.

As it turned out, I had actually already written down the hemlock formula years before. I got it from a book written by a woman who had helped her mother die after a battle with cancer. For some reason, I thought I might need it someday.

I knew my mother was slowing down because she had stopped watching television and listening to music. It was characteristic of her to want to take control of dying. I understood when she told me that she wanted to "be done with it." But I didn't want to give it to her unless I had to, and I would have done so only if she were ill—and she wasn't.

As it turned out, I didn't have to. She simply decided to stop eating and wait. I had her checked a number of times by her doctor, who gave her medication to help her sleep. Her last days were spent quietly.

On June 27, 1995, my mother died. I fully understood her choice, yet it was hard for me to picture life without her. I was devastated. In some ways, my mother's death was even harder than Bud's or my father's. Although Toni and Kathy mourned the loss of their grand-mother, their grief was mostly for me. To them, she had been an aloof woman with a lot of rules for them to follow. She was so much more to me, and I have never really gotten over the loss. I would continue to feel loss in different ways for years to come.

Concern for Kathy

On a beautiful summer morning in 1996, Kathy, her friend Linda, and I were standing in line at the Art Institute of Chicago, waiting to see the special Monet exhibition. Kathy looked very pale. She said she felt as if she was coming down with the flu. Because she was leaving for St. Louis that afternoon, I suggested that she see a doctor as soon as she got home. She agreed but ended up going to see her optometrist first because she already had an appointment.

The optometrist was astounded at Kathy's high blood pressure. It was so high that he expressed surprise that she hadn't had a stroke. He told her to have it checked out immediately. Shocked and alarmed, Kathy went to her doctor right away and from there to the hospital, where it was discovered that she was suffering from kidney failure.

She had no apparent warning. We were shocked until we did research and discovered that Kathy's previous doctor had noted in her file to keep an eye on her for possible kidney issues. Because her doctor had never said a word to her—and subsequently moved away—she was completely unaware of the situation.

As it turned out, Kathy had presented with a number of symptoms, but like most people, she didn't know how to interpret them. She had terrible headaches that she attributed to early menopause. She had hiccups but just ignored them. She was extremely tired for the first time in her life. Finally, all of those classic symptoms of kidney failure resulted in a diagnosis. Her kidney function ceased immediately.

Kathy underwent peritoneal dialysis four times a day for one year—all by herself. The method, which removes waste from the blood as well as excess fluid that the kidneys are no longer capable of removing, is a form of dialysis that carries a risk of serious infection. Despite the difficult diagnosis and treatment, Kathy, typically upbeat, told Toni and me that she was sure she would have a kidney transplant in a year. She didn't want us to worry.

We, however, were doubtful that a transplant would come through so quickly. The waiting list was (and remains) very long. Yet, one year later, in 1997, Kathy underwent a successful kidney transplant. We all felt incredibly blessed when the kidney began to work immediately. I was so grateful that when I returned from St. Louis, where I was helping to care for her, I immediately offered my volunteer services to the board of the National Kidney Foundation of Illinois. There, I learned that those with diabetes, hypertension, and kidney disease usually have no idea anything is wrong with them. Neither did Kathy.

After Kathy received her kidney transplant, she was healthy, vibrant, and radiant. We were so thankful for the donation that saved her life.

Family Frustrations

With Kathy's crisis under control, our attention turned to the complicated relationship between Ted and Toni. Their mutual dislike for each other started having a more profound impact. Ted was not a favorite of Toni's, but for some reason her anger was directed at me instead. We had terrible arguments when we never had before. Using her negativity toward Ted as a catalyst to start battles with me, Toni was acting out in order to blow off steam, and it was unbearable. With Bud, Toni had never found fault, despite his failures as a father. When she focused her anger on me, while alternately loving and resenting her sister, I was pained and frustrated.

Despite her disappointment and angry outbursts, Toni continued to behave like a rescuer to Kathy. She had been especially concerned during Kathy's illness and even started to bail her sister out financially, frequently petitioning me on Kathy's behalf with requests: "Mom, I think you should get Kathy a new car; her car is really no good" or "Mom, you want to help Kathy with her teeth?" Once, Toni sold her own jewelry to pay for something that Kathy needed.

Despite trying times in their lives, Kathy and Toni stayed close and supported each other.

Worse than Toni's temper was the fact that she was right in many ways. My marriage, by this time, revealed itself to be more of a union of expedience and convenience for Ted than a true love story. He was quoted in *Chicago* magazine saying that I was such an ebullient person I could light up a room. Perhaps so, but I could not light up the face of my husband, and that was painfully obvious to me.

Still, we enjoyed plenty of good times, especially when we traveled around the world on university business. On one trip we went to Japan, Korea, India, and London in only fifteen days—make that *daze*. In Hong Kong I splurged and got us a room at the Regency. It was $670 a night, and Ted was so angry that he had to walk up and down the harbor to calm himself. He couldn't believe I would spend so much money on one night in a hotel. However, it was the most gorgeous room, with a wall of glass and gardenias, roses, and fruit everywhere, and I had wanted to create a lasting and special memory with my spouse. Although Ted was furious that I had spent the money, he seemed to enjoy it while we were there, and he exercised the bragging rights of having stayed in such a lavish room when we came back.

The same thing happened in Las Vegas. After my tennis accident, we had gone to "Sin City" and stayed at the Bellagio Hotel. Ted took one look at the Chihuly glass ceiling that I exclaimed to be "magnificent" and replied, "You don't know me. This is the most garish thing I ever saw." It was possible that he was right, that I didn't really know him, yet, once again, after a fabulous dinner and a few shows, Ted returned to Chicago boasting about the opulence of the Bellagio and its "garish" appointments.

I returned from Las Vegas and learned that I had a problem much bigger than my taste in art or my husband's finicky nature. After being put together with spit and glue, my orthopedic surgeon was concerned because my bones were not growing back. I needed a second surgery. The decision was devastating. On May 12, 2000, Dr. Wixson took out all of the plates and screws he had previously anchored in me and grafted a new hip joint that he attached to the bone with a long rod leading down my thigh.

The stress I had been under—the pain, convalescence, surgeries, Kathy's kidney, Ted—took its toll. Although the surgery went well, I had a heart attack the morning after.

At least I was in the right place! The doctors rushed to my room, where I was recovering from the surgery, and debated about how to save me. Seemingly not aware of my presence, they did it aloud as I was lying on the bed. "Am I going make it?" I piped up while they were evaluating my prognosis. "Because if not, I have sure had a hell of a good time."

An hour later, I was in a freezing surgery room waiting to get a stent placed into my heart. Before I was wheeled in, they gave me three pills to take. They were enormous, almost too big for a horse. I told them that I had made it to the age of eighty-one without taking any pills, and I was proud of it. I leered at the giant-size medication and was convinced I would not be able to get the medicine down. The doctors told me that it was my decision: either take the pills and live or toss the pills and never leave the operating room. I took the pills.

Even with the fantastically skilled doctors doing their best work, I had complications after the surgery, and I remained in the hospital on oxygen for four weeks. Toni and Kathy took turns staying the night with me in my room. Ted was angry—and nowhere to be found. I think he felt a loss of control, so his answer was to give up and disconnect. He didn't appreciate the girls at all, and, in fact, I think he was even somewhat jealous that they were tending to me with so much care and concern. We all just seemed to be a nuisance to him.

Lying in bed was difficult enough in itself, but watching my girls fight day in and day out with Ted was more than I could bear, especially because I couldn't do anything about it. I was weak and knew I shouldn't get upset. Toni was angry. Kathy was scared. Ted was resentful. It was a trilogy of pain that I couldn't let myself get involved in without sacrificing my survival.

When it came time to go home, I was presented with a new set of worries. I was scared. I couldn't walk and needed somebody to take care of me. Ted wasn't offering any help and didn't know why the woman who cleaned the house couldn't do it. Nonplussed by his indifference and lack of compassion, I took the initiative to hire a caregiver for myself.

Ted took me home two days after our ninth wedding anniversary. As he pushed me, in my second wheelchair in two years, into the elevator of our building and into our apartment, he was eerily quiet. Instead of being kind, supportive, or warm, he was annoyed. His unfriendliness was not hard to miss. I was so relieved to be home that I ignored the fears piercing my heart and my soul. Once inside, Ted presented me with a lovely welcome home "get-well" gift: a letter he had written a few days prior.

Stunned but not quite knowing what to expect, I opened the envelope and was confronted by a litany of his displeasures. In essence, the letter said that he felt we should live separately until I recovered. He suggested that I go to live with Toni and predicted that we all would get along better that way. He even proposed that he and I could go out together now and then. As for his never-ending conflicts with my daughters, he also stated that he would refuse to let them visit me as long as he and I lived in the apartment together.

I was dismayed by the details of his proposition but truly horrified by his timing. I recall thinking, "How upset am I allowed to get?" At that point, I didn't know how much my heart could take. Being upset was only part of it; I was consumed by shock, betrayal, and anger.

Despite the emotions that were erupting, my response to his letter was deliberate and evenly measured. I patiently reminded Ted that I had just had major surgery as well as a heart attack. I told him that we could talk about the letter in a month. However, despite the calm and collected outside appearance I was displaying, the whole thing had such an immediately devastating effect on me that right then and there I decided privately that I wanted to be done with my marriage. My hurts, pains, and wounds were mortal. I didn't want to live with Ted any longer. I didn't want to be with him. Ever.

My daughters circled the wagons emotionally and pragmatically. Kathy found Donnie Schiller, one of the top divorce lawyers in the city, and Toni began to pull all of my paperwork together. Donnie's staff came to my home to meet with me. I'll never forget him telling me, "You are allowed what is fair under the law." I didn't want drama; I just wanted to do what was necessary and be done. I wasn't interested in Ted's retirement funds. The only thing I was anxious about was keeping my home.

As I healed and quietly planned the divorce, Ted and I continued to live together, and occasionally I even went out with him socially, as much as I could with my physical—and emotional—limitations. I was not able to walk for three long months while the graft took hold, and that meant that I had to be in a wheelchair 24-7. While Ted had always claimed that our twelve-year age difference didn't bother him and marveled that I kept up with him with the energy of a young girl, when he was with me in a wheelchair, he looked at me with the pained expression of a resentful caretaker. Although he never acknowledged this out loud, it was obvious with every gesture. It made me feel old, probably for the first time in my life.

Our marriage was disintegrating more every day. I tried my best to focus on getting well while ignoring the ongoing strife with Ted. It was sad, but I didn't want to argue; I had no intention of changing my mind—and anything I did would do nothing to change his. We had had an interesting life, enjoyed our travels, and met fascinating people along the way. Together, we had accomplished a great deal for Roosevelt. It was time to close the chapter and go on with the rest of my life.

At the end of September, a secretary in my attorney's office accidentally sent some confidential information to Ted's fax machine instead of mine. I regretted that he found out about my plans to divorce him that way, yet it was no less cruel than being handed a letter requesting a separation while being wheeled into the apartment after a strenuous fight to regain my health and mobility. Ted brought the fax to the dinner table and asked, "What the hell is this 'divorce' business?"

"I want one," I told him matter-of-factly. By then I had everything in order and was more at ease than I had been in months.

"What will I do?" he asked. "You have friends—I don't!"

"You'll get remarried," I replied. I made an accurate prediction, as it turns out.

Worried about what people would think, Ted suggested that we give it three months and then talk again. I agreed to wait, but by the end of that waiting period, nothing had changed, and I informed him that I wanted to proceed. That was when the real nastiness began. Ted retained Herb Lieberman to represent him. Herb was a successful divorce lawyer who would be a good match for my top gun, Donnie Schiller. We knew it would be a showdown, even though Herb had been a social acquaintance. The process was difficult, but he remained pleasant throughout it all.

Ted and I continued living together in the apartment for six more months. I was confined for a good deal of that time, but Ted began to go out even more than his usual hectic schedule necessitated. On Saturdays he would get dressed up in nice sweaters I had bought for him and go out for lunch. I knew he was seeing someone, and I even knew who it was, but none of it mattered anymore. He didn't, however, move out of our bedroom until Valentine's Day in 2001. This little present was a big gift.

As soon as I graduated from a walker to a cane, I was able to get back to work for the university. Interestingly enough, I have to say that during our divorce proceedings, as hard as it was living with Ted, working with him was actually harder. Because I was chairman of the Chicago Board, I went to senior board meetings and sat across the table from him, wondering who this man I had married and once loved was. He was quite unpleasant at my board meetings, so eventually I stopped inviting him.

On Monday, October 3, 2001, we were granted a divorce. Ted got remarried the following Sunday. There was so much I liked about him, and I thought we could make a go of it together, but it turned out I was wrong. In the end, he was the cold man I always knew him to be. I always regretted that Ted basically forbid his family to communicate with me after our divorce. I had continued to have a close relationship with Bud's family after his passing, but Ted had less of a sense of the importance of the family ties that bind.

The Unthinkable

As if the divorce hadn't been upsetting enough, instead of improving, my relationship with Toni continued to be traumatic. The absence of her nemesis, Ted, made no difference. Her tirades were continual and public. Kathy was so concerned about it that she called me from St. Louis every night to make sure I was OK.

Toni began to have health issues of her own. Earlier, she had had a breast reduction, during which doctors found that she had breast cancer in situ. The news was devastating. When she shared it with me, I had my own struggle. At the time I had tickets to attend a benefit with Ted, and he insisted that we go, against my wishes and motherly instinct to comfort my daughter in her moment of need.

Against her doctor's advice, Toni decided to have a prophylactic double mastectomy, a path many women opt for today but one that was a shockingly new course of treatment then. The pathology report showed that she already had cancer in four lymph nodes, so it was good that she had made peace with the mastectomy and didn't take any chances. However, the lymph node involvement caused her to have to endure more treatment. She tolerated the chemotherapy as best she could, lost her hair, wore wigs, and tried to go on as normally as possible, until the chemotherapy intensified her menopausal symptoms of hot flashes.

For years after her surgery, she was in remission but endured debilitating hot flashes that drained her emotionally. She became drenched in sweat every half hour. Even though she knew that hormone replacement therapy (also known as HRT) was a risk factor for breast cancer, she couldn't stand the intensity of the hot flashes anymore and decided to risk it. Our deepest fears came true when the cancer returned. In addition, the radiation she endured caused a previous bout of shingles to reactivate with enormous discomfort. She was in constant excruciating pain.

As Toni got sicker, she asked to move in with me. At first, I said no. I just couldn't imagine the difficulties of living with her temper. But upon a deeper reflection, I reached into my heart and said yes. She was my daughter—no matter how difficult she was. She needed care, and I wanted to be the one to provide it, as her mother. Toni moved in with me in 2004 in the spring. We quickly learned to adapt to each other's moods and made an effort to get along.

My relationship with Toni was complex, but she was my daughter, and I loved her dearly.

I cared for Kathy as she endured her illness and cherish the moments we spent together.

Just as Toni´and I were settling into our new life together, we were confronted by another crisis when Kathy was diagnosed with lung cancer. For three months, she kept the catastrophic news to herself. She was well aware that Toni had been fighting a cancer of her own and didn't want to worry us further. But on December 9, Kathy called from the hospital in St. Louis to tell me that she had pneumonia.

When I got to the hospital and saw exactly how sick Kathy was, I was aghast. In addition to her pneumonia, she was being given radiation for the lung cancer I didn't know she had until that moment. It seemed to me that radiation was unnecessary when she was so sick, but she had a cocky young doctor who wouldn't even consider altering his treatment.

I stayed in St. Louis and visited Kathy daily in the hospital. After undergoing an MRI that had detained her in Chicago, Toni joined us. She took one look at Kathy and announced that her sister should be in hospice. Her doctor refused to consider it, let alone recommend it.

I got permission to take Kathy home for Christmas. Her boss, Mr. Bly, who owned Ethan Allen Furniture, where Kathy worked part time, helped us transport her to her house. We got her upstairs, and I had to sleep with Kathy because she had only one enormous bed, plus a convertible couch in the den, where Toni slept. She was not feeling well herself at that point.

Those nights were terrible. Kathy lay in my arms and wept because she didn't want to die. She knew that she was seriously ill even though her doctor kept telling her that he was going to make her better. By that time, she wasn't interested in eating and was drinking Ensure for energy. She cried continuously. I was truly heartbroken to feel my child sobbing and could do little but hold her.

Our experiences during the next week were strange. I would wake up, not feel her next to me, and call out, "Kathy, where are you?" She was attached to an oxygen tank and had to be careful not to trip if she walked around. I found her sitting on a chair in a little room between her bedroom and her bathroom that she had used when she was on dialysis. Another night when she wasn't in bed next to me, I found her halfway up the steps, having gone down to the kitchen alone. "I tried to grind coffee and messed everything up," she said weakly. Then she attempted to get back up to bed but made it only halfway up the steps and lost her strength. Toni and I finally got her in bed. Lying next to her, I somehow managed not to cry.

Toni did what she could to help but was fighting her own illness. We felt it was so wrong that Kathy wasn't being provided hospice, but her stubborn doctor insisted that she continue the radiation. It hurt her and made her weak. It did not seem to be helping her at all, as the cancer had already spread. I asked Kathy whether I could call her internist, and she finally agreed. Dr. Sherry Shuman arranged for an MRI, and her former boss, Hugh Plunkett, came over and took us to the doctor's office, where Dr. Shuman told us that it was over. Kathy had the "luxury" of hospice for three days before she died. She washed her hair and had a manicure and a few visitors, giving her cat to one of them. She seemed to be at peace and even gave me permission to look for the baby she had given up so long ago. Her strength was gone, but her will to live was not.

On January 5, 2005, I was so exhausted from everything I could hardly stay awake any longer. Toni promised to keep an eye on Kathy while I slept. When I awoke at about 5:00, the house was eerily quiet. I knew Kathy was gone.

Her death was devastating for me and equally so for her sister. The next morning we began to arrange for Kathy's funeral and made our way back to Chicago from St. Louis. We were very lucky to be able to fly in because a snowstorm was developing and by the next day it was difficult to get around and many flights were canceled.

Despite our tremendous grief, we managed to plan the funeral. Together we selected Kathy's casket, as painful as it was. She had always told me that she pictured for herself a burial at sea, but in the depths of her sickness, one day she told me in a serious tone that she wanted to be in the family vault in Rosehill Cemetery, with all of us. Kathy was buried in our mausoleum next to Bud. We dressed her, per her request, in her "uniform": white jeans, white shirt, sweater, and clogs.

My friends offered an outpouring of support: Stan Lewin printed the programs, and David Hiller, the publisher of the *Chicago Tribune*, made it possible for us to print a large obituary for Kathy. In a short time, we put together a fitting tribute to Kathy and her indelible spirit.

Toni's Time

Toni and I went back to a life without Kathy and managed to get along. Somehow, being together seemed to temper the incredible sadness; we enjoyed having each other around, and the winter passed quickly. When spring came, we went for a walk along the lake, and halfway back Toni suddenly collapsed with a broken hip. Fortunately, a gentleman passing by helped lift her into a cab. Once upstairs at home, she was in a great deal of discomfort and pain. I called 911, and the ambulance took us to Northwestern Memorial Hospital. I stayed by her side during the whole ordeal. After a few days, we went home, and she recovered quite quickly and had therapy to improve her walking.

What a shame for her to have to suffer with this on top of the ongoing shingles pain and menopause—plus the cancer. One evening she was terribly uncomfortable and partially dehydrated. I made another call to 911, but this time Northwestern was closed to all patients, so she was taken to Rush-Presbyterian-St. Luke's that evening. My cousins Joan and Dick Mandel came and stayed with me at 2 a.m., which was a blessing. The cancer had spread to Toni's bones, and she was suffering a great deal.

Finally, Toni's oncologist, Dr. Janet Wolter, came in after reading the CAT scan and urged us to call hospice. We went home a few days before Thanksgiving and tried to enjoy the holiday as best we could. Instead of having a traditional dinner for a large crowd, Toni wanted it to be just for us. I ordered our meal from the Women's Athletic Club, and we enjoyed a nice Thanksgiving dinner just the two of us, mother and daughter.

Toni started to get confused and her behavior began to change because the cancer eventually affected her brain. After living with the disease for more than thirteen years, she was slowly losing her strength and her battle. With her deteriorating condition, I realized I needed some assistance. Anna Tomaschewski, a lovely Polish caregiver sent to me by my cousin Sally Salzer, arrived a couple of days after Thanksgiving. She was truly an angel, and I couldn't have gotten through without her help. She seemed to understand all the pain I was going through and provided a shoulder I could lean on.

Toni's hospice nurse was wonderful as well. She came every day and monitored Toni's pain medication, increasing it as needed to ease her discomfort. We were able to have a small Christmas and generally went along from day to day, not knowing what each one would bring. As January passed, we saw a consistent change in Toni. She started to have difficulty speaking and soon couldn't form the words to communicate. I knew she was close to the end, and I stayed right with her, never leaving her side. For hours, I sat with her and held her hand. I spoke softly to her, and though she couldn't respond, I'm sure she understood everything I said. As she passed, she smiled the precious smile of a child. It was a wonderful gift, just for me. Then she was gone.

For the second time in not much more than a year, I started making plans to bury a daughter. I ordered a copy of Kathy's casket and dressed Toni in a Lanz nightgown and red socks. When she was buried, I included birthday cards and the ashes of her cat, Peanuts. The service was held in May Chapel at Rosehill Cemetery. Piano music accompanied the tribute, and a Souza march, one of Toni's favorite's, ended the touching ceremony as people exited.

In the eighty-seventh year of my life, both of my daughters had died. My friend Mary O'Leary came to be with me, and my family offered their comfort, but nothing seemed to help. Both of my children were gone, and the sadness shook me to my core. I really didn't give a damn about anything after that. My heart was broken.

For the first and only time in my life, I wondered whether I could keep going, whether the show really would go on. The fog and haze of my devastation enveloped my entire being as I sank into a deep depression. I was not used to the terrible feeling of emptiness. Because the girls had died so close together, I hardly had the time to grieve the loss of one before the other was gone, too.

However, as time went on, I realized I could not mourn forever and was able to talk myself out of the darkness of my momentary depression. I needed to get back to the thing that had carried me through many challenging moments in my life before—work.

My relationship with Toni grew stronger as we mourned Kathy's loss together. Caring for her in her time of need brought us closer still.

The Kidney Foundation

In honor of Kathy, I had spent nearly a decade on the board of the National Kidney Foundation of Illinois. My major accomplishment was the creation of the KidneyMobile. It visits schools, hospitals, and community organizations in Chicago to test people for diabetes, hypertension, and kidney disease. The idea of a traveling medical center on wheels was new and exciting, but no one quite knew what to think. At the time some people had crazy ideas that it should look like a hot dog or a kidney. I had advertising guru Stan Lewin draft some drawings of how I wanted it to look, and with the plans in hand, I began my search for funding.

In honor of Kathy's struggle, I spent many years on the board of the National Kidney Foundation of Illinois. The creation of the KidneyMobile was my crowning success. It screens for high blood pressure, diabetes, and kidney disease, and I sincerely hope it can save lives. Since its creation in 2005, more than twenty-seven thousand people have been screened by the mobile—of which an overwhelming 75 percent have received results in the abnormal range for at least one criterion.

I called Ann Lurie, a former pediatric nurse who was left with six children, aged five to fifteen, when her husband, Robert, died in 1990. He had been the partner of Sam Zell, owner of the Tribune Company. By the time I approached her for a donation to the KidneyMobile, Ann had already given away more than $100 million to redress some of the world's biggest problems, including world hunger, cancer, and inadequate health care. She also made sizable contributions to Children's Memorial Hospital. To this day, she's given more than $330 million to various worthy causes. Through her foundation, she conceived of and established a mobile medical clinic to treat rural villagers in Kenya, so she was very familiar with the KidneyMobile concept.

Ann was extremely responsive—and generous. She gave me $200,000 after one conversation, saying that she wanted to do more but was committed to enhancing her work in Kenya as well as endowing the extensive garden in Millennium Park. Sidney Port, founder of Lawson Products, was another generous benefactor. He responded immediately with a contribution.

Finally, I went all the way to Matt Zell, the son of Sam Zell. Matt had a child with kidney disease, and we had served briefly together on the kidney foundation board. Willa Lang, executive director of the foundation at the time, informed me that Matt had agreed to give $100,000 a year for three years, which covered the overall operating costs of the KidneyMobile. I was so grateful for his donation and truly felt compassion for what he was going through with his own child. With his generosity, we were well on our way to making a big difference.

In November of 2005, the KidneyMobile was launched as a joint partnership between the National Kidney Foundation and the University of Illinois at Chicago Medical Center. To date, the mobile has screened thousands of people in neighborhoods throughout the Chicago metropolitan area and the rest of the state.

The nurse who staffed the mobile was so good at what she was doing that I felt confident leaving the operation in her hands. I continued to keep in touch with the staff at the KidneyMobile for years after and was available whenever they needed my help or input. It was fulfilling to have started something new that could help so many people, and doing the positive work and making things better for others helped to ease the loss of my girls.

With my work at the kidney foundation and the KidneyMobile coming to an end, the pace of my life was beginning to slow down a bit. I was ready for some time off. After the finalization of my divorce from Ted and the death of both of my girls, I needed a respite, to collect my thoughts and reorganize my life. I had been so busy giving to other people, both personally and professionally, I didn't quite remember what it was like to look after only myself. However, the "me time" felt good, and I did continue working on various projects, such as the Garden Committee at the Lincoln Park Zoo, so I wasn't a complete do-nothing!

Adjusting to the new realities took some time, but I found my life was once again taking shape. During my break from benefits and fundraising, I began to really enjoy my time off. Being thoroughly retired was delicious! My friend Mary Dempsey, who had finally stepped down from her position as commissioner of the Chicago Public Library system, agreed. Maybe being retired wasn't such a bad thing after all!

I found the time to reconnect with friends, some of whom I hadn't seen for many years, and in the process began to discover what a truly small world it can sometimes be. For instance, my friend Pat Wright, from Oklahoma, informed me that a neighbor of mine was a figure from my past, Irwin Press, whom I had helped in my work at Reese to develop patient satisfaction questionnaires used throughout the medical community (he later developed the company Press Ganey). He was someone whom I hadn't seen for twenty-five years, and when Pat came to visit, we all enjoyed a lovely lunch together, filled with many memories.

Many more memories came flooding back as I looked forward to celebrating my ninetieth birthday and continuing this new phase of my life. I had done so much but felt there was still more to do, including reflecting on my accomplishments for my city, as well as myself and my family, and recognizing the many people who had made my life richer over the years.

Celebrating Ninety

When I was married to Bud, he preferred to have parties at home, especially when it came to birthdays, so I never had a proper birthday party outside my own house as an adult. Upon my ninetieth birthday, I figured it was time! With the help of my dear friends and neighbors Don Raney and Jaymes Richardson, I set out to plan a gala to end all galas. We chose for the location Lake Shore Country Club, and we sent out music-themed invitations to as many people as the club could hold—220—and I still feel that the guest list was on the small side. The group I did invite displayed the remarkable diversity of my life adventures throughout the city and included famous figures as well as my family.

For my ninetieth birthday, I planned a birthday celebration for 220 guests with the help of my dear friends and neighbors Don Raney (right) and Jaymes Richardson (left). I cherish the memories of this magical event!

How to seat such a varied and sundry group? I wanted to be able to integrate them all and encourage mingling, so I set up tables named after noted musicians, such as Lena Horne, Barbara Streisand, Frank Sinatra, Judy Garland, and Tony Bennett, and each guest chose his or her favorite musician and sat at the corresponding table. It was a success—everyone loved the idea! To continue the music theme, my good friend Stanley Paul, a well-known pianist, provided the live entertainment.

We served delicious food—anything but the ordinary chicken! Everyone enjoyed the chef's special recipe for sea bass, and the dinner was further complemented by gorgeous table arrangements and center-pieces of glowing candles and red roses in full bloom. The whole party was in red, my favorite color; I even wore a dress to match. Everyone had a wonderful time—especially me!

I cherished the sight of people from my past, present, and future all assembled together in the same place. In fact, my family was absolutely flabbergasted in the presence of so many eminent Chicago citizens. I had never really told them exactly what it was that I did in my life and career; they had a general sense of what I was doing but no idea of the high-powered circles I operated in or the amounts of money I had raised for such worthy causes. One of the wonderful things about my life, and the lives of many fund-raisers, is the ability to get to know society's fas-cinating movers and shakers. I have been privileged to count among my friends people who are legends in my time. The Simon clan enjoyed meeting Bill Kurtis, Donna LaPietra, Abby McCormick O'Neil, John and Abra Rockefeller Prentice Wilkin, Tom and Barbara Carr, John Gunn, and others. My Simon relatives have always been wonderfully supportive, and they were no less so for my big birthday. They continued their tradition of "showing up": if something bad happened, they were there, just as if something good happened, they were there, too.

In my honor, speeches were given by Ramsey Lewis, Kristi Peterson, and Stan Lewin, as well as a few relatives. Their kind words meant the world to me, as did the comments and memories shared by all the guests on small note cards, later formed by Marsha Goldstein into a book that I cherish to this day. I was truly touched by the outpouring of love. I was celebrating not only my birthday but also all the wonderful relationships, both personal and professional, that I've been fortunate enough to develop and enjoy throughout my years.

In lieu of gifts, people made donations to the Lincoln Park Zoo and the Chicago Botanic Garden. As a token of my appreciation, I gave all the guests a small bottle of champagne as they departed. I was truly gratified that the celebration went so well and was so much fun. The details and special touches made for an elegant and memorable celebration not just for me but also for everyone in attendance. Throughout my life, I've never made it a habit to discuss my age, but I guess now it's no longer a secret!

Reflections on Today

Some people might think I would have slowed down a bit after my ninetieth birthday—but those people obviously don't know me very well! Though at a somewhat more leisurely pace, my work is still going strong. On some days, my schedule is more packed than that of someone half my age! I love being on the run, going, doing, helping. May it always be this way.

I have continued my work with the Lincoln Park Zoo and serve as a Life Director and Life Trustee. As part of the Garden and Sculpture Committee, I am committed to keeping the zoo, a place that holds such a special place in my heart, a vibrant, thriving, and beautiful treasure of the city.

In 2009, I chaired what may have been my last benefit, for the Chicago Symphony Orchestra. The auction was a huge success, and we raised funds for musical programs as well as outreach and education. I am a continued member of the Auction Committee, the Auditions Committee, and the Musicians' Luncheon Committee.

I'm pleased and humbled to receive continued recognition for my life's adventures and the dedication to my work over the years. In the Summer 2011 issue of *The Core*, the college magazine of the University of Chicago, a lovely piece on my Betty Co-Ed experience was published. It can be seen online at http://thecore.uchicago.edu/Summer2011/ departments/IN-editors-note.shtml. There, a slideshow of photos shows the thrilling experience of my college years and my visit to the New York World's Fair. Bringing back the memories, and sharing them with others, is a pleasure I won't forget.

Also in 2011, I was honored as a founding member of the Society for Healthcare Consumer Advocacy (SHCA), part of the American Hospital Association. At the annual conference, which that year celebrated SHCA's fortieth anniversary, they featured a video interview with me. I loved discussing my involvement in the beginnings of patient care and representation and sharing some of my expertise and advice for success in the field.

My work with the National Kidney Foundation of Illinois has continued, as well, in a different and more personal way. After having been away from the organization for some time, I was recently contacted by the board because the foundation was hoping to raise money and thought my experience in that arena would be a great help. I also met with the recipient of a kidney donation who counsels others in need of transplants. His story was as inspiring as it was comforting. In addition, Kathy's legacy lives on through my work with the KidneyMobile. Seeing things come full circle is satisfying and reassuring.

I'm grateful that I've been able to accomplish important things for worthy organizations. It fills my heart with a sense of achievement and triumph for causes that need the help and deserve the support. I once joked with Joe Regenstein that it must have been so much fun to be him: when he wanted to give money to support a charity, he gave it! If I wanted to give, I had to go out and raise the money. I loved doing it, and I hope my actions on behalf of so many projects have helped make Chicago—and maybe even the world—a better place.

My life has been full! I have seen my share of good times and bad, but they've all made me who I am. I miss my girls every day. Caring for them in their final days remains the most difficult time in my life. As a gift, my friend Tula Aravanis, from Greece, treated me to a reading from a British spiritual medium, Annette Jennifer Jones, who communicated with the girls on the "other side" and sent me the details of their conversation in a lengthy e-mail. They are together in the afterlife. What a wonderful vision. I was thrilled to find out about their journey together and now feel more connected to my beloved daughters in their absence.

A memorial was constructed for the girls at the zoo. If you enter the zoo from Café Brauer and make a sharp turn, in a garden are a large boulder and two plaques for Kathy and Toni. A plaque in remembrance of my mother is affixed to an ancient tree that stands opposite the girls' memorial. As another tribute, Toni's name appears on a brick at the Chicago Botanic Garden.

I never thought I would be denied the pleasure of having grandchildren; I just accepted it as something I would be able to enjoy and something I would be quite good at. I searched for the child Kathy gave up for adoption but found out through the medium that he, too, had died, in an automobile accident at age twenty-four.

It makes me heartsick sometimes having to listen to all of my friends talk about their grandsons and granddaughters, what great schools they've gotten into, what wonderful things they're doing. I have learned to turn off the pain most of the time, but it's hard.

Instead, I have focused attention on the other young people in my life and with whom I have come into contact. Seeking to be an adviser to them has led to many meaningful mentoring relationships over the years. They have been especially rewarding in so many ways. For those starting out in their careers, I have served as a guide and a guru, giving advice, fostering connections, and being a beacon for many looking to replicate my success.

Do I think I'll ever stop working, stop doing, stop being involved? I don't think so. Indeed, the show must go on! If it's something I can do, I want to do it. I want to continue working for people in need and for the betterment of Chicago, the city I love. Staying involved keeps me active and young. My wish is for everyone to find passion in life. Through a bit of luck and a lot of hard work, I was able to make a difference and lead a profound and exciting life, and for that I will forever be thankful. You learn as you live, and I have learned so much.

Photo Credits

The publishers gratefully acknowledge the courtesy of the following individuals, photographers, publishers, institutions, newspapers, and corporations for the illustrations in this volume. Credits are listed from top to bottom and from left to right on their respective pages. All images are from the collection of Ms. Marion Simon.

xii Michael Coakes
12 Bruno Bernard
22 KAM Isaiah Israel Congregation
25 Hyde Park Academy High School
32 Don Castle
34 WGN News
37 Alan Tishman
39 Bud Simon
42 Newspaper clipping from the *Chicago Tribune*, 1939
46 Newspaper clipping from the *Boston Traveler*, 1939
101 Newspaper clippings from unknown source
102 Newspaper clipping from unknown source
103 Newspaper clipping from the *Chicago Tribune*, 1966
104 Newspaper clipping from unknown source
108 Lincoln Park Zoo
111 Lincoln Park Zoo
132 Newspaper clipping from unknown source
145 Michael Reese Hospital and Medical Center
147 Michael Reese Hospital and Medical Center
170 Roosevelt University
181 Magazine clipping from *The American Benefactor*, 1997
183 *Roosevelt Review*
196 The White House
214 National Kidney Foundation of Illinois
215 National Kidney Foundation of Illinois
218 Adam Noel

Center 7 John Reilly
Center 8 Michael Reese Hospital and Medical Center, National Kidney Foundation of Illinois

Cover Adam Noel
Inside back cover Edward D'Ancona